Synodical Measure 1969

Church Representation Rules

This publication states the Rules as at 1 January 2006

CHURCH HOUSE PUBLISHING

Church House Publishing
Church House
Great Smith Street
London SW1P 3AZ

ISBN 9780 7151 1050 8

1985 edition published December 1984
1990 edition published January 1990
1993 edition published July 1992
1995 edition published January 1995
1996 edition published April 1996
1997 edition published December 1997
2001 edition published May 2001
2004 edition published September 2003
2006 edition published January 2006

Copyright © The Archbishops' Council 1984, 1990, 1992, 1995, 1996, 1997, 2001, 2003, 2004, 2006
Index copyright © Meg Davies 2006

All rights reserved. No part of this publication may be reproduced or stored or transmitted by any means or in any form, electronic or mechanical, including photocopying, recording, or any information storage and retrieval system, without written permission which should be sought from the Copyright and Contracts Administrator, The Archbishops' Council, Church House, Great Smith Street, London SW1P 3AZ.

Typeset by RefineCatch Limited, Bungay, Suffolk
Printed and bound by Halstan & Co. Ltd, Amersham, Bucks

Contents

PART I CHURCH ELECTORAL ROLL — 1
Formation of Roll — 1
Revision of Roll and Preparation of New Roll — 3
Procedural provisions relating to entry and removal of names — 5
Certification of Numbers on Rolls — 6
Provision with Respect to Person whose Name is on Guild Church Roll — 6

PART II PAROCHIAL CHURCH MEETINGS AND COUNCILS — 7
ANNUAL MEETINGS — 7
Convening of Meeting — 8
Chairman — 9
Business — 9
Qualifications of persons to be chosen or elected by annual meetings — 11
Conduct of Elections at Annual Meetings — 12
Variation of method of election — 13
CONDUCT OF ELECTIONS OF CHURCHWARDENS — 14
PAROCHIAL CHURCH COUNCIL — 15
Members — 15
General Provisions relating to Parochial Church Councils — 17
Term of office — 17
Limitation on years of service — 18
Parishes with more than one Place of Worship — 18
Joint parochial church councils — 20
Team councils — 22
Group councils — 24
SPECIAL MEETINGS — 25
EXTRAORDINARY MEETINGS — 25

PART III DEANERY SYNODS — 26
Membership — 26
Election and choice of members — 28
Variation of Membership of Deanery Synods by Scheme — 29
Representation of Cathedral Clergy and Laity — 30
Procedure — 30
Diocesan Electoral Registration Officer — 31

PART IV DIOCESAN SYNODS — 32
Membership of Diocesan Synods — 32
Elections of Members of Diocesan Synods by Deanery Synods — 34

Variation of Membership of Diocesan Synods by Scheme	37
Procedure of Diocesan Synods	38

PART V HOUSE OF LAITY OF GENERAL SYNOD 40
MEMBERSHIP OF THE HOUSE OF LAITY 40
ELECTIONS OF MEMBERS 41
Number of Elected Members	41
Qualification of Elected Members	42
Electoral Areas	43
Conduct of Elections	43
Duties and Payment of Presiding Officers	46
Term of office of membership of General Synod and other bodies	47

EX-OFFICIO AND CO-OPTED MEMBERS OF THE HOUSE OF LAITY 47

PART VI APPEALS AND DISQUALIFICATIONS 49
ENROLMENT APPEALS 49
ELECTION APPEALS 50
Vacation of seat by Member ceasing to be Qualified for Election	54
Ex-officio Membership not to Disqualify for Election	56

PART VII SUPPLEMENTARY AND INTERPRETATION 57
Casual vacancies	57
Resignations	59
Notices	60
Constraints in Elections	60
Revocation and Variation of Rules, etc.	60
Special Provisions	61
Meaning of Minister, Parish and other words and phrases	63

APPENDIX I 65
SYNODICAL GOVERNMENT FORMS 65

APPENDIX II 77
GENERAL PROVISIONS RELATING TO PAROCHIAL CHURCH COUNCILS 77

SUPPLEMENTARY MATERIAL (not forming part of the Rules) 82
TEXTS OF SELECTED ENACTMENTS REFERRED TO IN THE RULES 82

NOTES 90

INDEX (by page number) 91

These Rules were authorised as Schedule 3 to the Synodical Government Measure 1969. The Rules are printed here as amended by the following legislation –

1 January 1974	Church Representation Rules (Amendment) Resolution 1973 (S.I. 1973 No. 1865)
1 May 1980	Church Representation Rules (Amendment) Resolution 1980 (S.I. 1980 No. 178)
2 July 1980	Diocese in Europe Measure 1980
1 January 1982 (in part) and 1 January 1983	Church Representation Rules (Amendment) (No. 2) Resolution 1981 (S.I. 1981 No. 1650)
1 November 1983	Church Representation Rules (Amendment) Resolution 1981 (S.I. 1981 No. 959)
1 January 1985	Church Representation Rules (Amendment) (No. 1) Resolution 1984 (S.I. 1984 No. 1039)
1 January 1985	Church Representation Rules (Amendment) (No. 2) Resolution 1984 (S.I. 1984 No. 1040)
1 January 1989	Patronage (Benefices) Measure 1986
1 January 1990	Church Representation Rules (Amendment) (No. 1) Resolution 1989 (S.I. 1989 No. 2094)
1 January 1990	Church Representation Rules (Amendment) (No. 2) Resolution 1989 (S.I. 1989 No. 2095)
1 January 1993	Care of Churches and Ecclesiastical Jurisdiction Measure 1991
1 February 1994	Priests (Ordination of Women) Measure 1993
1 January 1995	Church Representation Rules (Amendment) Resolution 1994 (S.I. 1994 No. 3118)
1 January 1996	Church Representation Rules (Amendment) Resolution 1995 (S.I. 1995 No. 3243)
1 May 1996	Team and Group Ministries Measure 1995
1 May 1996	Church Representation Rules (Amendment) Resolution 1995 (S.I. 1995 No. 3243)
1 May 1997	Church Representation Rules (Amendment) Resolution 1995 (S.I. 1995 No. 3243)
1 March 1998	Church Representation Rules (Amendment) Resolution 1998 (S.I. 1998 No. 319)
1 January 1999	National Institutions Measure 1998
Different dates for different cathedrals	Cathedrals Measure 1999

1 January 2000	Church Representation Rules (Amendment) Resolution 1999 (S.I. 1999 No. 2112)
1 January 2002	Churchwardens Measure 2001
1 January 2004	Synodical Government (Amendment) Measure 2003
1 August 2004 (in part), 1 January 2005 (in part) and 15 February 2005	Church Representation Rules (Amendment) Resolution 2004 (S.I. 2004 No. 1889)

PART I
CHURCH ELECTORAL ROLL

Formation of Roll

1. (1) There shall be a church electoral roll (in these rules referred to as 'the roll') in every parish, on which the names of lay persons shall be entered as hereinafter provided. The roll shall be available for inspection by bona fide inquirers.

(2) A lay person shall be entitled to have his name entered on the roll of a parish if he is baptised, of sixteen years or upwards, has signed an application form for enrolment set out in Appendix I of these rules and declares himself either –

(a) to be a member of the Church of England or of a Church in communion therewith resident in the parish; or

(b) to be such a member and, not being resident in the parish, to have habitually attended public worship in the parish during a period of six months prior to enrolment; or

(c) to be a member in good standing of a Church which subscribes to the doctrine of the Holy Trinity (not being a Church in communion with the Church of England) and also prepared to declare himself to be a member of the Church of England having habitually attended public worship in the parish during a period of six months prior to enrolment.

Provided that where a lay person will have his sixteenth birthday after the intended revision of the electoral roll or the preparation of a new roll but on or before the date of the annual parochial church meeting, he may complete a form of application for enrolment and his name shall be enrolled but with effect from the date of his birthday.

(3) Where a person resides in an extra-parochial place he shall be deemed for the purposes of these rules to reside in the parish which it abuts, and if there is any doubt in the matter a determination shall be made by the bishop's council and standing committee.

(4) A person shall be entitled to have his name on the roll of each of any number of parishes if he is entitled by virtue of paragraphs (2) and (3) of this rule to have his name entered on each roll; but a person whose name is

entered on the roll of each of two or more parishes must choose one of those parishes for the purpose of the provisions of these rules which prescribe the qualifications for election to a deanery synod, a diocesan synod or the General Synod or for membership of a parochial church council under rule 14(1)(f) or of a deanery synod under rule 24(6)(b).

(5) The roll shall, until a parochial church council has been constituted in a parish, be formed and revised by the minister and churchwardens (if any), and shall, after such council has been constituted, be kept and revised by or under the direction of the council. Reference in this rule to a parochial church council shall, so far as may be necessary for giving effect to these rules, be construed as including references to the minister and churchwardens (if any).

(6) Where a new parish is created by a pastoral scheme, the roll of that parish shall in the first instance consist –

(a) in the case of a parish created by the union of two or more former parishes, of the rolls of those parishes combined to form one roll;

(b) in any other case, of the names of the persons whose names are at the date of the coming into existence of the new parish entered on the roll of a parish the whole or any part of which forms part of the new parish and who are either resident in the new parish or have habitually attended public worship therein.

(7) The parochial church council shall appoint a church electoral roll officer to act under its direction for the purpose of carrying out its functions with regard to the electoral roll.

(8) The names of persons who are entitled to have their names entered upon the roll of the parish shall, subject to the provisions of these rules, be from time to time added to the roll. It shall be the duty of the electoral roll officer to keep the roll constantly up to date by the addition and removal of names as from time to time required by these rules and to report such additions and removals at the next meeting of the parochial church council. When additions and removals have been made by the electoral roll officer a list of such amendments shall be published by being exhibited continuously for not less than fourteen days on or near the principal door of every church in the parish and every building in the parish licensed for public worship in such manner as the council may appoint and the list shall contain notification of the right of appeal referred to in rule 43.

Provided that where the roll is published in a form which contains parts each relating to one or more churches or places of worship within the parish, the publication of such amendments to any part of the roll may be limited to the churches or places of worship to which that part relates.

(9) Subject to the provisions of this rule, a person's name shall, as the occasion arises, be removed from the roll, if he –

(a) has died; or

(b) becomes a clerk in Holy Orders; or

(c) signifies in writing his desire that his name should be removed; or

(d) ceases to reside in the parish, unless after so ceasing he continues, in any period of six months, habitually to attend public worship in the parish, unless prevented from doing so by illness or other sufficient cause; or

(e) is not resident in the parish and has not habitually attended public worship in the parish during the preceding six months, not having been prevented from doing so by illness or other sufficient cause; or

(f) was not entitled to have his name entered on the roll at the time when it was entered.

(10) The removal of a person's name from the roll under any of the provisions of these rules shall be without prejudice to his right to have his name entered again, if he has or acquires that right.

(11) The roll shall where practicable contain a record of the address of every person whose name is entered on the roll, but a failure to comply with this requirement shall not prejudice the validity of any entry on the roll.

Revision of Roll and Preparation of New Roll

2. (1) Except in a year in which a new roll is prepared, the roll of a parish shall be revised annually by or under the direction of the council. Notice of the intended revision in the form set out in section 2 of Appendix I to these rules shall be affixed by the minister or under his direction on or near the principal door of every church in the parish and every building in the parish licensed for public worship and remain so affixed for a period of not less than fourteen days before the commencement of the revision. The revision shall be completed not less than fifteen days or more than twenty-eight days before the annual parochial church meeting.

(2) Upon every revision all enrolments or removals from the roll which have been effected since the date of the last revision (or since the formation of

the roll, if there has been no previous revision) shall be reviewed, and such further enrolments or removals from the rolls as may be required shall be effected.

(3) After the completion of the revision, a copy of the roll as revised shall, together with a list of the names removed from the roll since the last revision (or since the formation of the roll, if there has been no previous revision), be published by being exhibited continuously for not less than fourteen days before the annual parochial church meeting on or near the principal door of the parish church in such manner as the council shall appoint. During the period while the copy is so exhibited any errors and omissions in the roll may be corrected but subject thereto and to the provisions of rule 1(2), no names shall be added to or removed from the roll during the period in any year between the completion of the revision and the close of the annual parochial church meeting.

(4) Not less than two months before the annual parochial church meeting in the year 2007 and every succeeding sixth year notice in the form set out in section 3 of Appendix I to these rules shall be affixed by the minister or under his direction on or near the principal door of every church in the parish and every building in the parish licensed for public worship and remain so affixed for a period of not less than fourteen days. On the affixing of the notice a new roll shall be prepared.

At every service held on each of the two Sundays within the period of fourteen days beginning with the date of the affixing of the notice or, in the case of a church in which no service is held on either of those Sundays, at every service held in that church on the first Sunday after that date the person conducting the service shall inform the congregation of the preparation of the new roll.

(5) The parochial church council shall take reasonable steps to inform every person whose name is entered on the previous roll that a new roll is being prepared and that if he wishes to have his name entered on the new roll he must apply for enrolment. No such steps need be taken with respect to any person whose name could be removed from the previous roll under rule 1(9).

(6) The new roll shall be prepared by entering upon it the names of persons entitled to entry under rule 1(2), and a fresh application shall be required from persons whose names were entered on the previous roll. A person whose name was so entered shall not be disqualified for entry on the new roll by reason only of his failure to comply with the conditions specified

in rule 1(2)(b) and (c), if he was prevented from doing so by illness or other sufficient cause, and the circumstances shall be stated on the application form. The preparation of the new roll shall be completed not less than fifteen days or more than twenty-eight days before the annual parochial church meeting.

(7) After the completion of the new roll, a copy shall be published by being exhibited continuously for not less than fourteen days before the annual parochial church meeting on or near the principal door of the parish church in such manner as the council shall appoint. During the period while the copy is so exhibited any errors and omissions in the roll may be corrected but subject thereto and to the provisions of rule 1(2) no names may be added to or removed from the roll during the period in any year between the completion of the new roll and the close of the annual parochial church meeting. On the publication of the new roll it shall come into effect and the previous roll shall cease to have effect.

(8) Upon the alteration of the boundaries of any parishes the parochial church council of the parish from which any area is transferred shall inquire from the persons resident in that area whose names are entered on the roll of the parish, whether they wish to have their names transferred to the roll of the other parish. The parochial church council shall remove the names of persons answering in the affirmative from its own roll and shall inform the parochial church council of the parish in which such persons now reside, which shall enter the names on its roll without any application for enrolment being required.

Procedural provisions relating to entry and removal of names

3. (1) When a person applying for enrolment on the roll of any parish signifies his desire that his name should be removed from the roll of any other parish, notice of that fact shall be sent by the parochial church council receiving the application to the parochial church council of that other parish.

(2) When the name of any person is removed from the roll of the parish owing to his having become resident in another parish, notice of that fact shall, whenever possible, be sent by the parochial church council of the first mentioned parish to the parochial church council of the last mentioned parish.

[(3)–(5) repealed.]

Certification of Numbers on Rolls

4. Not later than the 1st June the chairman, vice-chairman, secretary or church electoral roll officer of the parochial church council shall notify in writing the secretary of the diocesan synod of the number of names on the roll of each parish as at the date of the annual meeting and a copy of such notification shall be affixed at or near to the principal door of every church in the parish and every building licensed for public worship in the parish when notification is sent to the secretary of the diocesan synod, and shall remain so affixed for a period of not less than fourteen days.

[Provision with Respect to Person whose Name is on Guild Church Roll]‡

5. (1) A person whose name is entered on the roll of a guild church shall for the purpose of the provisions of these rules which prescribe the qualifications for election to a deanery synod, a diocesan synod or the House of Laity of the General Synod, or for membership of a deanery synod under rule 24(6)(b), be deemed to be a person whose name is on the roll of the parish in which the guild church is, and references in those provisions or in rule 1(4) to a person whose name is on the roll of a parish or on the roll of each of two or more parishes, and in rule 46 to entry on the roll of a parish, shall be construed accordingly.

(2) In this rule 'guild church' means a church in the City of London designated and established as a guild church under the City of London (Guild Churches) Acts 1952 and 1960.

---

‡ This header does not appear in the statutory text.

PART II
PAROCHIAL CHURCH MEETINGS AND COUNCILS

ANNUAL MEETINGS

6. (1) In every parish there shall be held not later than the 30th April in each year the annual parochial church meeting (hereafter in these rules referred to as 'the annual meeting').

(2) All lay persons whose names are entered on the roll of the parish shall be entitled to attend the annual meeting and to take part in its proceedings, and no other lay person shall be so entitled.

(3) A clerk in Holy Orders shall be entitled to attend the annual meeting of the parish and take part in its proceedings –

(a) if he is either beneficed in or licensed to the parish or any other parish in the area of the benefice to which the parish belongs; or

(b) if he is resident in the parish and is not beneficed in or licensed to any other parish[.] ‡

(c) if he is not resident in the parish and is not beneficed or licensed to any other parish, the parochial church council with the concurrence of the minister has declared him to be an habitual worshipper in the parish, such declaration being effective until the conclusion of the annual meeting in the year in which a new roll is prepared under rule 2 or his ceasing to be an habitual worshipper in the parish whichever is the earlier, but without prejudice to a renewal of such declaration; or

(d) if he is a co-opted member of the parochial church council in accordance with rule 14(1)(h).

(4) Without prejudice to paragraphs (2) and (3) of this rule –

(a) all the members of the team of a team ministry shall be entitled to attend, and take part in the proceedings of, the annual meeting of the

---

‡ The full stop in the statutory text appears in error and should be replaced by the word '; or'.

parish or each of the parishes in the area of the benefice for which the team ministry is established, and where the area of a group ministry includes the area of a benefice for which a team ministry is established, all the vicars in that ministry shall be entitled to attend, and take part in the proceedings of, the annual meeting of each of the other parishes in the area for which the group ministry is established;

(b) all the incumbents and priests in charge in a group ministry shall be entitled to attend, and take part in the proceedings of, the annual meeting of each of the parishes in the area for which the group ministry is established.

(5) Where two or more benefices are held in plurality and a team ministry is, or is to be, established for the area of one of those benefices, then, if a pastoral scheme provides for extending the operation of the team ministry, so long as the plurality continues, to the area of any other benefice so held, paragraph (4) of this rule shall have effect as if the references to the area of the benefice were references to the combined area of the benefices concerned.

Convening of Meeting

7. (1) The annual meeting shall be convened by the minister of the parish by a notice in the form set out in section 4 of Appendix I to these rules affixed on or near to the principal door of every church in the parish and every building licensed for public worship in the parish, for a period including the last two Sundays before the day of the meeting.

(2) The annual meeting shall be held at such place on such date and at such hour as shall be directed by the previous annual meeting, or by the parochial church council (which may vary any direction given by a previous annual meeting) or in the absence of any such direction as shall be appointed by the minister.

(3) During the vacancy of the benefice or curacy or when the minister is absent or incapacitated by illness or any other cause, the vice-chairman of the parochial church council, or if there is no vice-chairman, or if he is unable or unwilling to act, the secretary of or some other person appointed by that council shall have all the powers vested in the minister under this rule.

(4) The annual meeting shall be held at a place within the parish unless the parochial church council decide otherwise.

(5) The minister of a new parish created by a pastoral scheme, or, in the absence of the minister, a person appointed by the bishop, shall as soon as

possible after the scheme comes into operation convene a special parochial church meeting, and, subject to paragraph (6) of this rule, the provisions of these rules relating to the convening and conduct of the annual meeting shall apply to a special meeting convened under this paragraph.

(6) A special meeting so convened and held in the month of November or the month of December may, if the meeting so resolves, be for all purposes under these rules the annual meeting for the succeeding year, and a special meeting so convened shall in any event be for all such purposes the annual meeting for the year in which it is so convened and held.

Chairman

8. (1) The minister, if present, or, if he is not present, the vice-chairman of the parochial church council, or, subject to paragraph (2) of this rule, if he also is not present, a chairman chosen by the annual meeting shall preside thereat.

(2) Where a parish is in the area of a benefice for which a team ministry is established, and a vicar in that ministry is entitled to preside at an annual meeting of that parish by virtue of a provision in a pastoral scheme or the bishop's licence assigning to the vicar the duties, or a share in the duties, of the chairmanship of the annual meeting of that parish, then, if both he and the vice-chairman of the parochial church council are not present at that meeting, but the rector in that ministry is present, the rector shall preside thereat.

(3) In the case of an equal division of votes, the chairman of the meeting shall have a second or casting vote, unless it is a case where rule 11(8) applies[.]‡ but no clerical chairman shall have a vote in the election of the parochial representatives of the laity.

Business

9. (1) The annual meeting shall receive from the parochial church council and shall be free to discuss –

(a) a report on changes in the roll since the last annual parochial church meeting or, in a year in which a new roll is prepared, a report on the numbers entered on the new roll;

(b) an annual report on the proceedings of the parochial church council and the activities of the parish generally;

---

‡ The full stop in the statutory text appears in error.

(c) the financial statements of the parochial church council for the year ending on the 31st December immediately preceding the meeting, independently examined or audited as provided by paragraph (3) hereof;

(d) a report upon the fabric, goods and ornaments of the church or churches of the parish, under section 5^1 of the Care of Churches and Ecclesiastical Jurisdiction Measure 1991; and

(e) a report on the proceedings of the deanery synod.

(2) The council shall cause a copy of the said roll to be available for inspection at the meeting.

(3) The said financial statements shall –

(a) be independently examined or audited in such manner as shall be prescribed in accordance with rule 54(8);

(b) be considered and, if thought fit, approved by the parochial church council and signed by the chairman presiding at the meeting of the council; and

(c) be displayed for a continuous period of at least seven days before the annual meeting, including at least one Sunday when the church is used for worship, on a notice-board either inside or outside the church.

(4) The annual report referred to in paragraph (1)(b) above and the said financial statements shall be prepared in such form as shall be prescribed in accordance with rule $54(8)^2$ hereof for consideration by the annual meeting. Following such meeting the council shall cause copies of the annual report and statements to be sent within twenty-eight days of the annual meeting to the secretary of the diocesan board of finance for retention by the board.

(5) The annual meeting shall in the manner provided by rule 11 –

(a) elect in every third year parochial representatives of the laity to the deanery synod;

(b) elect parochial representatives of the laity to the parochial church council;

(c) appoint sidesmen;

(d) appoint the independent examiner or auditor to the council for a term of office ending at the close of the next annual meeting, provided that such person shall not be a member of the council;

and the elections and appointments shall be carried out in the above order.

(6) Without prejudice to the foregoing provisions and rule 7(6), a special parochial church meeting convened under rule 7(5) shall, in addition to other business –

(a) decide on the number of members of the parochial church council who are to be the elected representatives of the laity;

(b) elect in the manner provided by rule 11 parochial representatives of the laity to the deanery synod, if such representatives are required to be elected in the year for which that meeting is the annual meeting by virtue of rule 7(6).

(7) Any person entitled to attend the annual meeting may ask any question about parochial church matters, or bring about a discussion of any matter of parochial or general church interest, by moving a general resolution or by moving to give any particular recommendation to the council in relation to its duties.

(8) The annual meeting shall have power to adjourn and to determine its own rules of procedure.

(9) The secretary of the parochial church council (or another person appointed by the meeting in his place) shall act as a clerk of the annual meeting, and shall record the minutes thereof.

Qualifications of persons to be chosen or elected by annual meetings

10. (1) Subject to the provisions of rule 1(4) and paragraph (3) of this rule, the qualifications of a person to be elected a parochial representative of the laity to either the parochial church council or the deanery synod are that –

(a) his name is entered on the roll of the parish and, unless he is under the age of eighteen years at the date of the election, has been so entered for at least the preceding period of six months;

(b) he is an actual communicant as defined in rule 54(1); and

(c) he is of sixteen years or upwards.

(2) The qualification of a person to be appointed a sidesman is that his name is entered on the roll of the parish.

(3) No person shall be nominated for election under rule 9 –

(a) to serve on either the parochial church council, or the deanery synod unless he has signified his consent to serve, or there is in the opinion of the meeting sufficient evidence of his willingness to serve;

(b) to serve on the parochial church council, if he has been disqualified under rule 46A[;]‡

[(c) repealed.]

Conduct of Elections at Annual Meetings

11. (1) Subject to the provisions of any resolution under rule 12 and for the time being in force this rule shall apply to all elections at annual meetings.

(2) All candidates for election at an annual meeting must be nominated and seconded by persons entitled to attend the annual meeting, and in the case of parochial representatives of the laity, by persons whose names are entered on the roll of the parish. A candidate shall be nominated or seconded either before the meeting in writing or at the meeting.

(3) If the number of candidates nominated is not greater than the number of seats to be filled, the candidates nominated shall forthwith be declared elected.

(4) If more candidates are nominated than there are seats to be filled, the election shall take place at the annual meeting.

(5) No clerk in Holy Orders shall be entitled to vote in the election of any parochial representatives of the laity.

(6) Each person entitled to vote shall have as many votes as there are seats to be filled but may not give more than one vote to any one candidate.

(7) Votes may be given –

(a) by show of hands, or

(b) if one or more persons object –
  (i) on voting papers signed by the voter on the reverse thereof; or
  (ii) if at least one tenth of the persons present and voting at the meeting so request, on numbered voting papers.

---

‡ The semi-colon in the statutory text appears in error.

(8)(a) Where owing to an equality of votes an election is not decided, the decision between the persons for whom the equal numbers of votes have been cast shall be taken by lot.

(b) When an election or any stage of an election is recounted, either on appeal or at the request of the presiding officer or of a candidate, if the original count and the re-count are identical at the point when a lot must be drawn to resolve a tie, the original lot shall be used to make the determination.

(9) The result of any election by an annual meeting shall be announced as soon as practicable by the person presiding over the election, and a notice of the result shall in every case be affixed on or near the principal door of every church in the parish and every building licensed for public worship in the parish, and shall bear the date on which the result is declared. The notice shall remain affixed for not less than fourteen days. Thereafter the secretary of the parochial church council shall hold a list of the names and addresses of the members of the council which shall be available for inspection on reasonable notice being given by any person who either is resident in the parish or has his name on the electoral roll, but the secretary shall not be bound to provide a copy of such list.

(10) Names and addresses of parochial representatives of the laity elected to the deanery synod shall be sent by the secretary of the parochial church council to the diocesan electoral registration officer appointed in accordance with rule 29 and to the secretary of the deanery synod.

(11) Where a vote is conducted in accordance with paragraph (7)(b)(ii) above, a record shall be made of the identity of each person to whom a numbered voting paper is issued and any such record, so long as it is retained, shall be kept separate from the voting papers.

Variation of method of election by scheme

12. (1) The annual meeting may pass a resolution which provides that the election of parochial representatives of the laity to the parochial church council or to the deanery synod or to both that council and that synod shall be conducted by the method of the single transferable vote under rules, with the necessary modifications, made by the General Synod under rule [39(7)]‡ and for the time being in force, except that where the vote is conducted in

---

‡ The correct cross-reference is to Rule 39(8).

accordance with Rule 11(7)(b)(ii), those rules shall have effect with the omission of any requirement that the voting paper be signed by the voter.

(2) The annual meeting may pass a resolution which provides that any person entitled to attend the annual meeting and vote in the elections of parochial representatives of the laity to the parochial church council or to the deanery synod or to both that council and that synod may make application in the form set out in section 4A of Appendix I for a postal vote.

(3) Where applications for postal votes have been received by the date specified in the notice convening the annual meeting and where the number of candidates nominated for an election referred to in paragraph (2) of this rule is greater than the number of seats to be filled, the annual meeting shall appoint a presiding officer who shall not be a candidate in the election. Voting papers shall be distributed to each person present at the meeting entitled to vote and completed papers shall be returned into the custody of the presiding officer before the close of the meeting. The presiding officer shall ensure that persons who have made application for a postal vote shall be sent or have delivered a voting paper within 48 hours of the close of the meeting such paper to be returned to the presiding officer within such period of not less than seven days nor more than fourteen days from the date of the meeting as the presiding officer shall specify.

(4) A resolution passed under this rule shall be invalid unless approved by at least two-thirds of the persons present and voting at the annual meeting nor shall it be operative until the next ensuing annual meeting. Such resolution may be rescinded by a subsequent resolution passed in the same manner.

CONDUCT OF ELECTIONS OF CHURCHWARDENS

13. (1) Elections of churchwardens under the Churchwardens Measure 2001[3] shall be conducted, announced and notified in the same manner as elections under rule 11, except that all persons entitled to attend the meeting of parishioners other than the minister shall be entitled to nominate and vote at such elections of churchwardens.

[(2) repealed.]

PAROCHIAL CHURCH COUNCIL

Members

14. (1) Subject to the provisions of rule 1(4) and paragraph (3) of this rule, the parochial church council shall consist of –

(a) all clerks in Holy Orders beneficed in or licensed to the parish, . . . ;

(aa) any clerk in Holy Orders who is duly authorised to act as chairman of meetings of the council by the bishop in accordance with paragraph 5(b) of Appendix II to these rules;

(b) any deaconess or lay worker licensed to the parish;

(c) in the case of a parish in the area of a benefice for which a team ministry is established, all the members of the team of that ministry;

(d) the churchwardens and any deputy churchwardens who are ex-officio members of the parochial church council by virtue of a scheme made under rule 18(4) of these rules, being actual communicants whose names are on the roll of the parish;

(e) such, if any, of the readers who are licensed to that parish or licensed to an area which includes that parish and whose names are on the roll of the parish as the annual meeting may determine;

(f) all persons whose names are on the roll of the parish and who are lay members of any deanery synod, diocesan synod or the General Synod;

(g) six representatives of the laity where there are not more than fifty names on the electoral roll, nine such representatives where there are not more than one hundred names on the roll and, where there are more than one hundred names on the roll, a further three such representatives for every one hundred (or part thereof) names on the roll up to a maximum of fifteen such members, and so that the aforesaid numbers "six", "nine", "three" and "fifteen" may be altered from time to time by a resolution passed at any annual meeting, but such resolution shall not take effect before the next ensuing annual meeting; and

(h) co-opted members, if the parochial church council so decides, not exceeding in number one-fifth of the representatives of the laity elected under the last preceding sub-paragraph of this paragraph, or two persons whichever shall be the greater, and being either clerks in Holy Orders or actual lay communicants of sixteen years of age or upwards. The term of office of a co-opted member shall be until the conclusion of the next annual meeting; but without prejudice to his being co-opted on subsequent occasions for a similar term, subject to and in accordance with the provisions of these rules.

(2) Any person chosen, appointed or elected as a churchwarden of a parish, being an actual communicant whose name is on the roll of the parish, shall as from the date on which the choice, appointment or election, as the case may be, is made be a member of the parochial church council of the parish by virtue of this paragraph until he is admitted to the office of churchwarden, and he shall thereafter continue to be a member of that council by virtue of paragraph 1(d) of this rule unless and until he ceases to be qualified for membership by virtue of that sub-paragraph.

(3) A person shall cease to be a member of a parochial church council –

(a) if his name is removed from the roll of the parish under rule 1, on the date on which his name is removed;

(b) if he refuses or fails to apply for enrolment when a new roll is being prepared, on the date on which the new roll is completed;

(c) if he is or becomes disqualified under Rule 46A, from the date on which the disqualification takes effect;

but, so far as the provisions of (a) and (b) above are concerned, shall be without prejudice to any right which that council may have to make that person a co-opted member.

(4) Where a group ministry is established the incumbents of all benefices in the group every priest in charge of any benefices therein and where the area of the group ministry includes the area of a benefice for which a team ministry is established, all the vicars in that ministry shall be entitled to attend meetings of the parochial church councils of all the parishes in the area for which the group ministry is established. They shall be entitled to receive documents circulated to members of councils of which they are not themselves members and to speak but not to vote at meetings of such councils.

(5) Where two or more benefices are held in plurality and a team ministry is, or is to be, established for the area of one of those benefices, then, if a pastoral scheme provides for extending the operation of the team ministry, so long as the plurality continues, to the area of any other benefice so held, paragraphs (1)(c) and (4) of this rule shall have effect as if the references to the area of the benefice were references to the combined area of the benefices concerned.

General Provisions relating to Parochial Church Councils

15. The provisions in Appendix II to these rules shall have effect with respect to parochial church councils, and with respect to the officers, the meetings and the proceedings thereof:

Provided that a parochial church council may, with the consent of the diocesan synod, vary the said provisions, in their application to the council.

Term of office

16. (1) Subject to the following provisions of these rules, representatives of the laity serving on the parochial church council by virtue of rule 14(1)(g) shall hold office from the conclusion of the annual meeting at which they were elected until the conclusion of the third annual meeting thereafter, one third retiring and being elected each year, but, subject to rule 17, shall on retirement be eligible for re-election.

(2) Where a representative of the laity resigns or otherwise fails to serve for his full term of office the casual vacancy shall be filled for the remainder of his term of office in accordance with rule 48(1).

(3) Notwithstanding the preceding provisions of this rule an annual meeting may decide that the representatives of the laity serving by virtue of rule 14(1)(g) shall retire from office at the conclusion of the annual meeting next following their election, but any such decision shall not affect the terms of office as members of the parochial church council of those due to retire from office at the conclusion of an annual meeting held after that at which the decision was taken.

(4) A decision taken under paragraph (3) above shall be reviewed by the annual meeting at least once every six years; and on any such review the annual meeting may revoke the decision, in which case paragraph (1) above shall apply unless and until a further decision is taken under paragraph (3).

(5) Persons who are members of a parochial church council by virtue of their election as lay members of a deanery synod shall hold office as members of the council for a term beginning with the date of their election and ending with the 31st May next following the election of their successors.

(6) At an annual meeting at which all the representatives of the laity

serving by virtue of rule 14(1)(g) are elected to hold office in accordance with paragraph (1) above, lots shall be drawn to decide which third of the representatives is to retire in the first year following that in which the meeting is held, which third is to retire in the second year and which third is to retire in the third year.

Limitation on years of service

17. The annual meeting may decide that no representative of the laity being a member of the parochial church council by virtue of rule 14(1)(g) may hold office after the date of that meeting for more than a specified number of years continuously and may also decide that after a specified interval a person who has ceased to be eligible by reason of such decision may again stand for election as representative of the laity on the council.

Parishes with more than one Place of Worship

18. (1) In any parish where there are two or more churches or places of worship the annual meeting may make a scheme, which makes provision for either or both of the following purposes, that is to say: –

(a) for the election of representatives of the laity to the parochial church council in such manner as to ensure due representation of the congregation of each such church or place; and

(b) for the election by the annual meeting for any district in the parish in which a church or place of worship is situated of a district church council for that district.

(2) A scheme for the election of any district church council or councils under the preceding paragraph shall provide for the election of representatives of the laity on to such council, for ex-officio members and for the chairmanship of such council and shall contain such other provisions as to membership and procedure as shall be considered appropriate by the annual meeting.

(3) Such a scheme may also provide for the delegation by the parochial church council to a district church council of such functions as may be specified in the scheme and, subject to the provisions of the scheme, the parochial church council may be resolution also delegate to a district church council such of its functions as it shall think fit but not including (in either case) the functions of the parochial church council –

(i) in respect of producing the financial statement of the parish . . . ;

(ii) as an interested party under Part I of the Pastoral Measure 1983;
(iii) under Part II of the Patronage (Benefices) Measure 1986;
(iv) under section 3 of the Priests (Ordination of Women) Measure 1993.

(4) A scheme may provide for the election or choice of one or two deputy churchwardens . . . , and for the delegation to him or them of such functions of the churchwardens relating to any church or place as the scheme may specify, and the churchwardens may, subject to the scheme, delegate such of their said functions as they think fit to the deputy churchwarden or churchwardens. The scheme may also provide for the deputy churchwardens to be ex-officio members of the parochial church council.

(5) No scheme under this rule shall be valid unless approved by at least two-thirds of the persons present and voting at the annual meeting nor shall the scheme provide for it to come into operation until such date as the bishop's council and standing committee may determine being a date not later than the next ensuing annual meeting. Every such scheme shall on its approval be communicated to the bishop's council and standing committee of the diocesan synod which may determine –

(a) that the scheme shall come into operation; or

(b) that the scheme shall not come into operation; or

(c) that the scheme shall come into operation with specified amendments, if such amendments are approved by an annual or special parochial church meeting and the scheme as amended is approved by at least two-thirds of the persons present and voting at that meeting.

[(5A) repealed.]

(6) A special parochial church meeting of a parish to which this rule applies may be convened for the purpose of deciding whether to make such a scheme . . . , and where such a meeting is convened the foregoing provisions shall have effect with the substitution for references to the annual meeting of references to the special meeting.

(7) Where a pastoral scheme establishing a team ministry, or an instrument of the bishop made by virtue of that scheme, makes, in relation to a parish in the area of the benefice for which the team ministry is established, any provision which may be made by a scheme under this rule, no scheme under this rule relating to that parish shall provide for the scheme to come into operation until on or after the date on which the provisions in question of the

pastoral scheme or of the instrument, as the case may be, cease to have effect.

(8) A scheme under this rule may be amended or revoked by a subsequent scheme passed in accordance with the provisions of paragraph [(4)]‡ of this rule.

(9) Every member of the team of a team ministry shall have a right to attend the meetings of any district church council elected for any district in a parish in the area of the benefice for which the team ministry is established.

(10) This rule shall be without prejudice to the appointment, in parishes with more than one parish church, of two churchwardens for each church under section 27(5) of the Pastoral Measure 1983.

(11) In this rule 'place of worship' means a building or part of a building licensed for public worship.

Joint parochial church councils

19. (1) Where there are two or more parishes within the area of a single benefice or two or more benefices are held in plurality, the annual meetings of all or some of the parishes in the benefice or benefices may make a joint scheme to provide –

(a) for establishing a joint parochial church council (hereinafter referred to as 'the joint council') comprising the ministers of the parishes and such numbers of representatives of each of those parishes elected by and from among the other members of the parochial church council of the parish as may be specified in the scheme;

(b) for the chairmanship, meetings and procedure of the joint council;

(c) subject to paragraph 20 of Schedule 2 to the Patronage (Benefices) Measure 1986 for the delegation by the parochial church council of each such parish to the joint council of such of its functions, other than its functions as an interested party under Part I of the Pastoral Measure 1983 and its functions under section 3 of the Priests (Ordination of Women) Measure 1993, as may be so specified.

(2) Subject to the scheme and to any pastoral scheme or order made under paragraph 13 of Schedule 3 to the said Measure and to paragraph 20

---

‡ The correct cross-reference should be to paragraph (5).

of Schedule 2 to the Patronage (Benefices) Measure 1986, the parochial church council of any such parish may delegate to the joint council such of its functions, other than its functions as an interested party under the said Part I and its functions under section 3 of the Priests (Ordination of Women) Measure 1993, as it thinks fit.

(3) The joint council shall meet from time to time for the purpose of consulting together on matters of common concern.

(4) No scheme under this rule shall be valid unless approved by at least two-thirds of the persons present and voting at the annual meeting nor shall the scheme provide for it to come into operation until such date as the bishop's council and standing committee may determine being a date not later than the next ensuing annual meeting. Every such scheme shall on its approval be communicated to the bishop's council and standing committee of the diocesan synod which may determine –

(a) that the scheme shall come into operation; or

(b) that the scheme shall not come into operation; or

(c) that the scheme shall come into operation with specified amendments, if such amendments are approved by an annual or special parochial church meeting and the scheme as amended is approved by at least two-thirds of the persons present and voting at that meeting.

(5) A special parochial church meeting of a parish to which this rule applies may be convened for the purpose of deciding whether to join in making such a scheme, and where such a meeting is convened the foregoing provisions shall have effect with the substitution for references to the annual meeting of references to the special meeting.

(6) Where a pastoral scheme or order, or any instrument of the bishop made by virtue of such a scheme or order, establishes a joint parochial church council for two or more of the parishes in a single benefice or two or more of the parishes in benefices held in plurality, no scheme under this rule relating to those parishes shall provide for the scheme to come into operation until on or after the date on which the provisions of the pastoral scheme, pastoral order or instrument, as the case may be, establishing the joint parochial church council cease to have effect.

(7) Where the provisions of a pastoral scheme or order for the holding of benefices in plurality are terminated under section 18(2) of the Pastoral Measure 1983, any provision of a scheme under this rule establishing a joint

parochial church council for all or some of the parishes of those benefices and the other provisions thereof affecting that council shall cease to have effect on the date on which the first mentioned provisions cease to have effect.

(8) A scheme under this rule may be amended or revoked by a subsequent scheme passed in accordance with the provisions of paragraph (4) of this rule [to be]‡.

Team councils

20. (1) Where a team ministry is established for the area of a benefice which comprises more than one parish the annual meetings of the parishes in that area may make a joint scheme to provide –

   (a) for establishing a team council comprising –

   (i) the team rector;

   (ii) the members of the team other than the team rector;

   (iii) every assistant curate, deaconess and lay worker licensed to a parish within the team who are not members of the team;

   (iv) such number of lay representatives elected by and from among the lay representatives of the parochial church council of each parish in the area as may be specified in the scheme.

   Provided that where the total number of persons in sub-paragraphs (ii) and (iii) above would otherwise number more than one-quarter of the total membership of the team council they may, and where those persons number more than one-third they shall select among themselves which members shall be members of the team council so that the total number of those persons shall not exceed more than one-third of the council.

   (b) for the chairmanship, meetings and procedure of the team council; and

   (c) subject to paragraph 19 of Schedule 2 to the Patronage (Benefices) Measure 1986 for the delegation by the parochial church council of each such parish to the team council of such functions, other than its functions as an interested party under Part I of the Pastoral Measure

---

‡ The words 'to be' appear in error in the statutory text.

1983, as may be so specified and its functions under section 3 of the Priests (Ordination of Women) Measure 1993, as may be so specified.

(2) Subject to the scheme and to any pastoral scheme relating to the team council made under paragraph 4(3) of Schedule 3 to the said Measure and to paragraph 19 of Schedule 2 to the Patronage (Benefices) Measure 1986, the parochial church council of any such parish may delegate to the team council such of its functions, other than its functions as an interested party under the said Part I and its functions under section 3 of the Priests (Ordination of Women) Measure 1993, as it thinks fit.

(3) The team council shall meet from time to time for the purpose of consulting together on matters of common concern.

(4) No scheme under this rule shall be valid unless approved by at least two-thirds of the persons present and voting at the annual meeting nor shall the scheme provide for it to come into operation until such date as the bishop's council and standing committee may determine being a date not later than the next ensuing annual meeting. Every such scheme shall on its approval be communicated to the bishop's council and standing committee of the diocesan synod which may determine –

(a) that the scheme shall come into operation; or

(b) that the scheme shall not come into operation; or

(c) that the scheme shall come into operation with specified amendments, if such amendments are approved by an annual or special parochial church meeting and the scheme as amended is approved by at least two-thirds of the persons present and voting at that meeting.

(5) A special parochial church meeting of a parish to which this rule applies may be convened for the purpose of deciding whether to join in making such a scheme, and where such a meeting is convened the foregoing provisions shall have effect with the substitution for references to the annual meeting of references to the special meeting.

(6) Where a pastoral scheme establishing a team ministry, or an instrument of the bishop made by virtue of that scheme, establishes a team council for that ministry, no scheme under this rule relating to that ministry shall provide for the scheme to come into operation until on or after the date on which the provisions of the pastoral scheme or of the instrument, as the case may be, establishing the team council cease to have effect.

(7) A scheme under this rule may be amended or revoked by a

subsequent scheme passed in accordance with the provisions of paragraph (4) of this rule [to be]‡.

Group councils

21. (1) Where a pastoral scheme establishes a group ministry, the annual meetings of the parishes in the area for which the group ministry is established may make a joint scheme to provide –

    (a) for establishing a group council comprising –

        (i) all the members of the group ministry,

        (ii) every assistant curate, deaconess and lay worker licensed to any such parish, and

        (iii) such number of lay representatives elected by and from among the lay members of the parochial church council of each such parish as may be specified in the scheme;

    (b) for the chairmanship, meetings and procedure of the group council; and

    (c) for the delegation by the parochial church council of each such parish to the group council of such functions, other than its functions as an interested party under Part I of the Pastoral Measure 1983 and its functions under Part II of the Patronage (Benefices) Measure 1986 and section 3 of the Priests (Ordination of Women) Measure 1993, as may be so specified.

(2) If the area of a group ministry includes the area of a benefice for which a team ministry is established, a scheme under this rule shall provide for the vicars in that ministry, as well as the rector, and all the other members of the team to be members of the group council.

(3) Paragraphs (2) to (7) of rule 20 shall apply in relation to a scheme under this rule as they apply in relation to a scheme under that rule with the modification that for the references to a team ministry and a team council there shall be substituted references to a group ministry and a group council respectively except that the functions of a parochial church council under Part II of the Patronage (Benefices) Measure 1986 and section 3 of the Priests (Ordination of Women) Measure 1993 may not be delegated to a group council.

---

‡ The words 'to be' appear in error in the statutory text.

SPECIAL MEETINGS

22. (1) In addition to the annual meeting the minister of a parish may convene a special parochial church meeting, and he shall do so on a written representation by not less than one-third of the lay members of the parochial church council; and the provisions of these rules relating to the convening and conduct of the annual meeting shall, with the necessary modifications, apply to a special parochial church meeting.

(2) All lay persons whose names are entered on the roll of the parish on the day which is twenty-one clear days before the date on which any special parochial church meeting is to be held shall be entitled to attend the meeting and to take part in its proceedings, and no other lay person shall be so entitled.

(3) A clerk in Holy Orders shall be entitled to attend any such meeting and to take part in its proceedings if by virtue of rule 6(3), (4) or (5) he would have been entitled to attend the annual meeting of the parish had it been held on the same date, and no other such clerk shall be so entitled.

EXTRAORDINARY MEETINGS

23. (1) On a written representation made to the archdeacon by not less than one-third of the lay members of the parochial church council, or by one-tenth of the persons whose names are on the roll of the parish, and deemed by the archdeacon to have been made with sufficient cause, the archdeacon shall convene an extraordinary meeting of the parochial church council or an extraordinary parochial church meeting, and shall either take the chair himself or shall appoint a chairman to preside. The chairman, not being otherwise entitled to attend such meeting, shall not be entitled to vote upon any resolution before the meeting.

(2) In any case where the archdeacon is himself the minister, any representation under paragraph (1) of this rule shall be made to the bishop, and in any such case the references to the archdeacon in paragraph (1) of this rule shall be construed as references to the bishop, or to a person appointed by him to act on his behalf.

(3) Paragraphs (2) and (3) of rule 22 shall apply in relation to an extraordinary parochial church meeting under this rule as they apply in relation to a special parochial church meeting under that rule with the modification that for the word 'special' in paragraph (2) of that rule there shall be substituted the word 'extraordinary'.

PART III
DEANERY SYNODS

Membership

24. (1) A deanery synod shall consist of a house of clergy and a house of laity.

(2) The members of the house of clergy of a deanery synod shall consist of –

(a) the clerks in Holy Orders beneficed in or licensed to any parish in the deanery;

(b) any clerks in Holy Orders licensed to institutions in the deanery under the Extra-Parochial Ministry Measure 1967;

(c) any clerical members of the General Synod or diocesan synod resident in the deanery;

(d) such other clerks in Holy Orders holding the bishop's licence to work throughout the diocese or in more than one deanery and resident in the deanery subject to any direction which may be given by the members of the house of clergy of the bishop's council that, having regard to the number of parochial and non-parochial clergy in the deanery, such clerk shall have membership of a specified deanery synod other than the deanery where he resides provided that no person shall thereby be a member of more than one deanery synod in the diocese;

(e) one or more clerks in Holy Orders holding permission to officiate in the diocese who are resident in the deanery or who have habitually attended public worship in a parish in the deanery during the preceding six months. One clerk may be elected or chosen for every ten such clerks or part thereof, elected or chosen in such manner as may be approved by the bishop by and from such clerks.

(3) Where an extra parochial place is not in a deanery it shall be deemed for the purposes of these rules to belong to the deanery which it abuts and if there is any doubt in the matter a determination shall be made by the bishop's council and standing committee.

(4) For the purposes of paragraph 2(e) of this rule the relevant date shall be the 31st December in the year immediately preceding any election of the

parochial representatives of the laity, and as soon as possible after that date the rural dean of the deanery shall inform the bishop of the number of clerks in Holy Orders who are qualified for membership of the deanery synod by virtue of that sub-paragraph.

(5) Not later than the 1st July following the election of parochial representatives of the laity to the deanery synod the secretary of the said synod shall send to the diocesan electoral registration officer appointed in accordance with rule 29 a list of the names and addresses of the members of the house of clergy, specifying the class of membership, and shall keep the said officer informed of subsequent changes in membership.

(6) Subject to the provisions of rule 1(4), the members of the house of laity of a deanery synod shall consist of the following persons, that is to say –

(a) the parochial representatives elected to the synod by the annual meetings of the parishes of the deanery;

(b) any lay members of the General Synod a diocesan synod or an area synod constituted in accordance with section 17 of the Dioceses Measure 1978 whose names are entered on the roll of any parish in the deanery;

(c) if in the opinion of the bishop of the diocese any community of persons in the deanery who are in the spiritual care of a chaplain licensed by the bishop should be represented in that house, one lay person, being an actual communicant member of the Church of England of sixteen years or upwards, chosen in such manner as may be approved by the bishop by and from among the members of that community;

(d) the deaconesses and lay workers licensed by the bishop to work in any part of the deanery;

(e) such other deaconesses or lay workers holding the bishop's licence to work throughout the diocese or in more than one deanery and resident in the deanery subject to any direction which may be given by the members of the House of Laity of the bishop's council that, having regard to the number of deaconesses or lay workers in the deanery, such person shall have membership of a specified deanery synod other than the deanery where they reside provided that no person shall thereby be a member of more than one deanery synod in the diocese.

(7) The house of clergy and house of laity of a deanery synod may co-opt additional members of their respective houses, being clerks in Holy Orders or, as the case may be, lay persons who shall be actual communicant members of the Church of England of sixteen years or upwards:

Provided that the number of members co-opted by either house shall not exceed five per cent of the total number of members of that house or three, whichever is the greater.

The names and addresses of co-opted members shall be sent by the secretary of the deanery synod to the diocesan electoral registration officer appointed in accordance with rule 29.

Election and choice of members

25. (1) ... The parochial representatives of the laity elected by annual meetings shall be so elected every three years, and shall hold office for a term of three years beginning with the 1st June next following their election.

(2) The numbers to be so elected from the several parishes shall be determined by resolution of the diocesan synod not later than the 31st December in the year preceding any such elections, and those numbers shall be calculated by reference to the numbers of names on the rolls of the parishes as certified ... under rule 4 or the number of parish churches or districts in each parish or a combination of both such methods, in each case in such manner as the diocesan synod shall determine provided that such resolution shall not make it possible for a parish with fewer than twenty-six names on the roll to have more than one representative.

(3) Not later than the 31st December in the year preceding any such elections, the secretary of the diocesan synod shall certify to the secretary of each parochial church council the number of such representatives to be elected at the annual meeting of the parish ... and shall send to the secretary of each deanery synod copies of the certificates and information relating to the parishes of the deanery.

(4) ... Any person to be chosen as mentioned in rule 24(2)(e) or 24(6)(c) shall be so chosen every three years and shall hold office for a term of three years beginning with the 1st June next following the date on which he is so chosen.

(5) A direction by the appropriate members of the bishop's council making provision under rule 24(2)(d) or 24(6)(e) for the membership of the clerks in Holy Orders or the deaconesses or lay workers therein mentioned may provide for the choice by a class of such persons of some of their number to be members, and for the term of office of persons so chosen.

(6) The diocesan synod shall exercise their powers under this and the last preceding rule so as to secure that the total number of members of any

deanery synod in the diocese shall not be more than 150 and, so far as practicable, shall not be less than 50:

Provided that the maximum number of 150 may be exceeded for the purpose of securing that the house of laity is not less in number than the house of clergy.

For the avoidance of doubt it is hereby declared that the number of 150 specified in this paragraph includes the maximum number of members who may be co-opted by each house.

Variation of Membership of Deanery Synods by Scheme

26. (1) If it appears to the diocesan synod that the preceding rules in this Part relating to the membership of deanery synods ought to be varied to meet the special circumstances of the diocese or the deaneries and to secure better representation of clergy or laity or both on the deanery synods, they may make a scheme for such variation, and, if the scheme comes into operation under this rule, the said rules shall have effect subject to the scheme.

(2) Copies of every such scheme must be sent to members of the diocesan synod at least fourteen days before the session at which they are considered, and every such scheme shall require the assent of the house of bishops and of a two-thirds majority of the members of each of the other houses of the synod present and voting.

(3) A scheme approved by the diocesan synod as aforesaid shall be laid before the General Synod.

(4) If a member of the General Synod gives notice in accordance with the Standing Orders of that Synod that he wishes such a scheme to be debated, the scheme shall not come into operation unless it is approved by the General Synod.

(5) If no notice is given under paragraph (4) of this rule with respect to any such scheme, or such notice having been given, the scheme is approved by the General Synod, it shall come into operation on the day after the end of the group of sessions during which it was laid before, or approved by, the General Synod or on such later date as may be specified in the scheme.

Representation of Cathedral Clergy and Laity

27. (1) Any diocesan synod may provide by scheme for the representation on such deanery synod as may be determined by or under the scheme –

(a) of the dean or provost, the residentiary canons and other ministers of the cathedral church of the diocese, or any of them; and

(b) in the case of a cathedral church which is not a parish church, of lay persons who are on the roll of members of the cathedral community (hereinafter in these rules referred to as "the community roll") required to be kept under section 9 of the Cathedrals Measure 1999 or, in the case of Westminster Abbey, St George's Chapel, Windsor and the cathedral church of Christ in Oxford, who are declared by the dean to be habitual worshippers at the cathedral church and whose names are not entered on the roll of any parish.

(2) The provisions of rule [21(2)]‡ shall apply to schemes made under this rule.

Procedure

28. (1) The diocesan synod shall make rules for deanery synods which shall provide –

(a) that the rural dean and a member of the house of laity elected by that house shall be joint chairmen of the deanery synod and that they shall agree between them who shall chair each meeting of the synod or particular items of business on the agenda of the synod;

(b) that there shall be a secretary of the deanery synod;

(c) that a specified minimum number of meetings shall be held by the deanery synod in each year;

(d) that on such matters and in such circumstances as may be specified in the rules, voting shall be by houses, but that otherwise decisions shall be taken by a majority of the members of the synod present and voting;

(e) that there shall be a standing committee of the synod with such membership and functions as the rules may provide;

(f) that the synod shall prepare and circulate to all parochial church councils in the deanery a report of its proceedings;

---

‡ The correct cross-reference should be Rule 26(2).

and may provide for such other matters consistent with these rules as the diocesan synod think fit.

(2) Subject to any such rules, the deanery synod shall have power to determine its own procedure.

Diocesan Electoral Registration Officer

29. (1) In every diocese, there shall be a diocesan electoral registration officer who shall be appointed by the bishop's council and standing committee of the diocesan synod and who shall record the names and addresses of all members of the house of clergy and house of laity of the deanery synods in the diocese in two registers (in these rules respectively referred to as 'the register of clerical electors' and 'the register of lay electors'); the members co-opted to the house shall be listed separately in the appropriate register.

(2) The diocesan electoral registration officer shall not later than twenty-one days before the nomination papers are circulated send a copy of the names and addresses of clerical electors and lay electors as recorded by him to the secretary of the deanery synod of which those electors are members and the secretary of the deanery synod shall within seven days of receipt certify in writing to the electoral registration officer that the names and addresses are correct or notify him in writing of any necessary corrections.

(3) The diocesan electoral registration officer shall, not later than seven days before nomination papers are circulated, send a copy of the corrected names and addresses of electors to the appropriate presiding officer in the election.

PART IV
DIOCESAN SYNODS

Membership of Diocesan Synods

30. (1) A diocesan synod shall consist of a house of bishops, a house of clergy and a house of laity.

(2) The members of the house of bishops shall consist of the bishop of the diocese, every suffragan bishop of the diocese and such other person or persons, being a person or persons in episcopal orders working in the diocese, as the bishop of the diocese, with the concurrence of the archbishop of the province, may nominate.

(3) The bishop of the diocese shall be the president of the diocesan synod.

(4) The members of the house of clergy shall consist of –

(a) the following ex-officio[1] members, that is to say –

    (i) any person or persons in episcopal orders nominated by the bishop of the diocese, other than a suffragan bishop or a person nominated under paragraph (2) of this rule;

    (ii) the dean or provost of the cathedral (including in appropriate dioceses, the Dean of Westminster, the Dean of Windsor and the Deans of Jersey and Guernsey);

    (iii) the archdeacons;

    (iv) the proctors elected from the diocese or from any university in the diocese (the University of London being treated for this purpose as being wholly in the diocese of London) to the Lower House of the Convocation of the Province, . . . ;

    (v) any other member of that House, being the person chosen by and from among the clerical members of religious communities in the Province, who resides in the diocese;

    (vi) the chancellor of the diocese (if in Holy Orders); and

    (vii) the chairman of the diocesan board of finance and the chairman of the diocesan advisory committee (if in Holy Orders);

(b) members elected by the houses of clergy of the deanery synods in the diocese in accordance with the next following rules; and

(c) not more than five members (being clerks in Holy Orders) co-opted by the house of clergy of the diocesan synod.

(5) The members of the house of laity shall consist of –

(a) the following ex-officio[2] members, that is to say –

  (i) the chancellor of the diocese (if not in Holy Orders);

  (ii) the chairman of the diocesan board of finance and the chairman of the diocesan advisory committee (if not in Holy Orders);

  (iii) the members elected from the diocese to the House of Laity of the General Synod, . . . ;

  (iv) any other member of that House, being an ex-officio or co-opted member of the House of Laity of the General Synod or a person chosen by and from among the lay members of religious communities in the Province, who resides in the diocese;

(b) members elected by the houses of laity of the deanery synods in the diocese in accordance with the next following rules; and

(c) not more than five members co-opted by the house of laity of the diocesan synod, who shall be actual communicants of sixteen years or upwards.

(6) The bishop of the diocese may nominate ten additional members of the diocesan synod, who may be of the clergy or the laity and shall be members of the appropriate house. Except in regard to their appointment the nominated members shall have the same rights and be subject to the same rules as elected members. Where necessary the bishop's council and standing committee shall designate the deanery synod of which the nominated member shall be a member and, where a nominated lay person is on more than one electoral roll, he shall choose the parochial church council of which he is to be a member.

(7) No person shall be entitled to be a member of more than one diocesan synod at the same time except –

(a) the chancellor of the diocese;

(b) a suffragan bishop appointed to act as a provincial episcopal visitor for the purposes of the Episcopal Ministry Act of Synod 1993 who, in addition to membership of the diocesan synod of the diocese of which he is suffragan, may be invited by the bishop of the diocese where he resides to be a member of that diocesan synod in accordance with paragraph (2) or paragraph (4)(a)(i) of this rule provided that he shall exercise his vote on a matter referred by the General Synod under Article 8 of the Constitution[3] only in the diocesan synod of the diocese of which he is suffragan.

(8) The registrar of the diocese and any deputy registrar of the diocesan synod shall be disqualified from standing for election to the diocesan synod or from being a nominated, co-opted or ex-officio member of that synod.

Elections of Members of Diocesan Synods by Deanery Synods

31. (1) The elections of members of the diocesan synods by the houses of clergy and laity of the deanery synods in the diocese shall take place every three years, and the members so elected shall hold office for a term of three years beginning with the 1st August next following their election.

(2) Any clerk in Holy Orders who is a member of the deanery synod ... shall be qualified to be so elected by the house of clergy of a deanery synod, and the electors shall be those whose names and addresses are recorded in the register of clerical electors being the persons referred to in rule 24(2) and not including the persons co-opted to the deanery synod under rule 24(7).

Provided that no clerk shall stand for election by more than one deanery synod.

(3) Subject to the provisions of rule 1(4), any lay person who is an actual communicant as defined in rule 54(1) of sixteen years or upwards and whose name is entered on the roll of any parish in the deanery or who is on the community roll or, in the case of Westminster Abbey, St George's Chapel, Windsor and the cathedral church of Christ in Oxford, declared by the dean to be an habitual worshipper at the cathedral church shall be qualified to be so elected by the house of laity of a deanery synod, and the electors shall be those whose names and addresses are recorded in the register of lay electors other than persons co-opted to the deanery synod under rule 24(7).

[proviso repealed.]

(4) The qualifying date for electors under paragraphs (2) and (3) of this rule and when a casual vacancy is being filled shall be 6.00 a.m. on the date on which the nomination papers are issued in accordance with rule 32(4).

(5) The register of clerical electors and the register of lay electors shall be open to inspection at the diocesan office and any errors and omissions in the list may be corrected until the close of nominations. Thereafter no names may be added or removed until the declaration of the result of the election and those persons whose names are entered in the register shall be the qualified electors entitled to vote in that election.

(6) The diocesan synod shall, not later than the 31st December in the year preceding any such election, determine the numbers of members to be so elected by the houses of the several deanery synods in the diocese, and the numbers shall –

(a) in the case of elections by the houses of clergy, be related to the numbers of members of those houses in the respective deanery synods;

(b) in the case of elections by the houses of laity, be related to the total numbers of names on the rolls of the parishes in the respective deaneries as certified . . . under rule 4:

Provided that at least two members shall be elected by each house of every deanery synod.

(7) For the purpose of such determination by the diocesan synod, the secretary of every deanery synod shall, not later than the 1st June, certify to the secretary of the diocesan synod the number of members of the house of clergy of the synod as at the 30th April.

(8) The diocesan synod shall so exercise their powers under this rule as to secure that the number of members of the synod is not less than 120 and not more than 270 and that the numbers of the houses of clergy and laity are approximately equal.

[proviso repealed.]

For the avoidance of doubt it is hereby declared that the number 270 specified in this paragraph includes the maximum number of members who may be co-opted by each house or nominated by the bishop.

(9) Not later than the 31st December in each year preceding any such elections, the secretary of the diocesan synod shall certify to the secretary of every deanery synod the numbers determined under this rule for that deanery synod.

32. (1) Elections of members of the diocesan synod by the houses of the deanery synods shall be completed by the 15th day of July, the period and dates of the election being fixed by the bishop of the diocese and communicated to the secretaries of the deanery synods.

(2) The bishop shall appoint the presiding officers for the elections by the houses of the deanery synods, provided that no person shall be appointed as a presiding officer for an election by a house . . . of which he is a member. The expenses of elections shall be paid out of diocesan funds.

(3) The diocesan electoral registration officer shall furnish the presiding officer with the names and addresses of the qualified electors and the presiding officer shall ensure that the persons qualified to nominate and vote in elections to the diocesan synod, and only such persons, shall be sent or given nomination and voting papers in respect of the said election at the address entered against their names in the register of electors.

(4) Every candidate must be nominated and seconded by a qualified elector. A notice in the form set out in section 5 of Appendix I indicating the number of seats to be filled and inviting nominations shall be despatched to every elector together with a form of nomination in the form set out in section 6 of Appendix I shall be delivered either by post, by facsimile transmission or in person to the presiding officer of the area within such period, being a period of not less than fourteen days ending on a date specified by the presiding officer, provided that where a nomination paper has been sent by facsimile transmission the name of the candidate shall not appear on the voting paper unless the original nomination paper has been received by the presiding officer within three days of the closing date for nominations. The nomination form shall be accompanied by a statement signed by the candidate stating his willingness to serve if elected and, if he so desires, setting out in not more than 100 words a factual statement for circulation with the voting papers of the candidate's professional qualifications, present office and any relevant past experience.

(5) It shall be the duty of the presiding officer –

(a) to scrutinise nomination papers as soon as they have been lodged and shall, without delay, inform the candidate concerned whether the nomination is valid. Where the nomination is invalid the presiding officer shall give his reasons for so ruling and if, by the close of the nomination period, no valid nomination is received, the candidate shall be excluded from the election;

(b) to supply free of charge to a duly nominated candidate in the election one copy of the names and addresses of the qualified electors within seven days of receiving his written request.

(6) If more candidates are nominated than there are seats to be filled the names of the candidates nominated shall be circulated on a voting paper in

the form set out either in section 7 or in section 8 of Appendix I to every qualified elector. The diocesan synod shall, not later than the 31st December in each year preceding any such election as is referred to in rule 31, make a determination as to which form of voting paper is to be used by the deaneries in that election, and that determination shall apply to any election to fill a casual vacancy which occurs during the next ensuing three years.

(7) The voting paper marked and, on the reverse thereof, signed by the elector and with his full name written shall be returnable to the presiding officer within such period not being less than fourteen days as he shall specify ... No vote shall be counted if given on a voting paper not in accordance with this paragraph.

(8) Where voting papers in the form set out in section 7 of Appendix I have been used and owing to an equality of votes an election is not decided, the decision between the persons for whom the equal number of votes have been cast shall be taken by lot by the presiding officer.

(9) Where voting papers in the form set out in section 8 of Appendix I are used, the election shall be conducted under rules, with the necessary modifications, made by the General Synod under rule 39(7) and for the time being in force.

(10) A return of the result of the election shall be sent by the presiding officer to the secretary of the diocesan synod and a statement of the result shall be sent by the presiding officer to every candidate not later than the 1st August in each election year.

Variation of Membership of Diocesan Synods by Scheme

33. (1) If it appears to the diocesan synod that the preceding rules in this Part relating to the membership of diocesan synods ought to be varied to meet the special circumstances of the diocese and to secure better representation of clergy or laity or both on the diocesan synod, they may make a scheme for such variation, and if the scheme comes into operation in accordance with the provisions hereinafter applied, the said rules shall have effect subject to the scheme.

[*proviso repealed.*]

(2) Paragraphs (2) to (5) of rule 26 shall apply to schemes under this rule as it applies to schemes under that rule.

Procedure of Diocesan Synods

34. (1) The diocesan synod shall make standing orders which shall provide –

(a) that the bishop need not be chairman of its meetings if and to the extent that standing orders otherwise provide;

(b) that there shall be a secretary of the diocesan synod;

(c) that a specified minimum number of meetings being in the case of a diocese in which area synods have been constituted in accordance with section 17 of the Dioceses Measure 1978, not less than one, and in the case of any other diocese not less than two shall be held in each year;

(d) that a meeting of the diocesan synod shall be held if not less than a specified number of members of the synod so request;

(e) that subject to the three next following sub-paragraphs, nothing shall be deemed to have the assent of the diocesan synod unless the three houses which constitute the synod have assented thereto but that if in the case of a particular question (except a matter referred to the diocesan synod by the General Synod under the provisions of Article 8 of the Constitution[4]) the diocesan bishop (if present) so directs, that question shall be deemed to have the assent of the house of bishops only if the majority of the members of that house who assent thereto includes the diocesan bishop;

(f) that questions relating only to the conduct of business shall be decided by the votes of all the members of the diocesan synod present and voting, . . . ;

(g) that every other question shall be decided by the votes of all the members of the diocesan synod present and voting, the assent of the three houses being presumed, unless the diocesan bishop (if present) requires or any ten members require that a separate vote of each house be taken;

(h) that if the votes of the houses of clergy and laity are in favour of any matter referred to the diocesan synod by the General Synod under the provisions of Article 8 of Schedule 2 of this Measure,[5] that matter shall be deemed to have been approved for the purposes of the said Article;

(i) that where there is an equal division of votes in the house of bishops, the diocesan bishop shall have a second or casting vote;

(j) that the diocesan bishop shall have a right to require that his opinion on any question shall be recorded in the minutes;

(k) that there shall be a bishop's council and standing committee of the diocesan synod with such membership as may be provided by standing orders and with the functions exercisable by it under section 4(4)[6] of the Measure and such other functions as may be provided by the standing orders or by these rules or by any Measure or Canon;

and may contain such further provisions consistent with these rules as the diocesan synod shall consider appropriate.

(2) No person shall be entitled to serve as a member of more than one bishop's council and standing committee at the same time.

(3) The registrar of the diocese shall be the registrar of the diocesan synod, and may appoint a deputy.

PART V
HOUSE OF LAITY OF GENERAL SYNOD

[MEMBERSHIP OF THE HOUSE OF LAITY]‡

35. (1) The House of Laity of the General Synod shall consist of –

(a) the members elected by the diocesan electors of each diocese as hereinafter provided;

(b) two members chosen by and from the members of religious communities having their mother house in either province in such manner as may be provided by a resolution of the General Synod;

(c) such ex-officio and co-opted members as are hereinafter provided.

(d) not less than three nor more than four members elected or chosen in such manner as may be determined by the Forces Synodical Council as soon as practicable after any dissolution of the General Synod, being actual communicants, provided that the total number of persons elected or chosen to serve on the General Synod by virtue of this sub-paragraph, paragraph 1(d) of the provisions relating to the Convocation of Canterbury of Canon H 2 and paragraph 1(bb) of Canon H 3 shall not exceed seven.

(2) For the purposes of this Part of these rules the diocese in Europe shall be deemed to be a diocese in the Province of Canterbury.

(3) For the purposes of this Part of these rules, the diocesan electors of a diocese other than the diocese in Europe shall be the members of the houses of laity of all the deanery synods in the diocese other than:

(a) persons co-opted to the deanery synod under rule 24(7); or

(b) persons who are lay members of a religious community with separate representation in the General Synod under paragraph 1(b) of this rule.

---

‡ This header does not appear in the statutory text.

(4) The diocesan electors of the diocese in Europe shall be such number of persons elected by the annual meetings of the chaplaincies in the said diocese as may be determined by the bishop's council and standing committee of the said diocese, and any lay person who is:

(a) an actual communicant as defined in rule 54(1),

(b) of eighteen years or upwards, and

(c) a person whose name is entered on the electoral roll of such a chaplaincy,

shall be qualified for election as a diocesan elector by the annual meeting of that chaplaincy.

(5) The qualifying date for lay members of religious communities under paragraph (1)(b) of this rule and for diocesan electors under paragraphs (3) and (4) of this rule shall be 6.00 a.m. on the date of the dissolution of the General Synod, save that when a casual vacancy is being filled, the qualifying date shall be 6.00 a.m. on the date on which the nomination papers are issued.

(6) The register of lay electors shall be open to inspection at the diocesan office and any errors and omissions in the list may be corrected until the close of nominations. Thereafter no names may be added or removed until the declaration of the result of the election and those persons whose names are entered in the register shall be the qualified electors entitled to vote in that election.

ELECTIONS OF MEMBERS

Number of Elected Members

36. (1) The total number of members directly elected and specially elected from the dioceses in the Province shall not exceed 136 for Canterbury and 59 for York and no diocese shall have fewer than three directly elected members (except the diocese in Europe which shall elect two members, and the diocese of Sodor and Man which shall elect one member). The representatives of the religious communities referred to in rule 35(1)(b), the elected or chosen persons referred to in rule 35(1)(d), ex-officio and co-opted members (as defined in rule 42) shall be additional to the said total number.

In this rule the term 'specially elected' means . . . the representatives of the Channel Islands elected in accordance with the provisions of the Channel Islands (Representation) Measure 1931 and such persons shall be included in the said total number.

(2) The total number of members to be elected by the diocesan electors of all the dioceses shall be fixed by resolution of the General Synod not later than the last day of February in the fifth year after the last preceding election of the House of Laity (but subject as hereinafter provided), and the resolution shall apportion the number so fixed to the Provinces of Canterbury and York in a proportion of 70 to 30 or as nearly as possible thereto and shall divide the number among the dioceses (using such divisor method as may from time to time be specified for the purpose by the Business Committee of the General Synod) so that the number of members to be elected by the several dioceses are as nearly as possible proportionate to the total number of names on the rolls of the parishes of the diocese in question.

[(3) repealed.]

(4) The number of members of the House of Laity to be elected by each diocese, when fixed by the General Synod as aforesaid, shall forthwith be certified to the secretaries of the diocesan synods.

(5) If the General Synod is at any time dissolved . . . before the fixing of numbers under this rule by the General Synod . . . , the General Synod or the Presidents thereof may give directions with respect to the fixing and certifying of the numbers of members to be elected to the House of Laity by each diocese, and the directions may provide that the numbers so fixed and certified on the last previous occasion shall be deemed to have been fixed and certified for the purpose of the election following the dissolution, and the directions may, if the dissolution is known to be impending, be given before it occurs.

Qualification of Elected Members

37. (1) Subject to the provisions of rule 1(4) and of rule 46(A), a lay person shall be qualified for election for any diocese by the diocesan electors of the diocese if –

(a) he is an actual communicant as defined in rule 54(1) but as if, in that definition, for the words "whose name is on the roll of a parish and" there were substituted the word "who";

(b) he is of eighteen years of age on the date of the dissolution of the General Synod or, when a casual vacancy is being filled, on the date on which the nomination papers are issued in accordance with rule 39(3);

(c) his name is at 6.00 a.m. on the date of dissolution of the General Synod or, when a casual vacancy is being filled, on the date on which the nomination papers are issued in accordance with rule 39(3), entered on the roll of any parish in the diocese or, in the case of a cathedral which is not a parish church, on the community roll or, in the case of Westminster Abbey, St George's Chapel, Windsor and the cathedral church of Christ in Oxford is a person who at any time within the period of two months beginning one month immediately before that date is declared by the dean of the cathedral church to be an habitual worshipper at that cathedral church.

[(1A) repealed.]

[(2) repealed.]

(3) Where a diocese is divided into two or more areas in accordance with rule 38(2), any person who under this rule is qualified for election for the diocese shall be qualified for election for any such area whether or not the parish on whose roll his name is entered, or the cathedral church on whose community roll his name is entered, is situated in that area, but no person shall be nominated for more than one such area at the same time.

Electoral Areas

38. (1) Subject to any division of a diocese under this rule every diocese shall be an electoral area for the purposes of elections to the House of Laity.

(2) So far as is consistent with any rule made under the Standing Orders of the General Synod under rule 39(8) and subject to paragraph (3) of this rule, a diocesan synod may, for the purposes of any election, divide a diocese into two or more areas, and apportion the number of members of the House of Laity to be elected for the diocese among such areas, and the election shall be conducted in each area as if such area were a separate diocese. Where a diocese is so divided, a diocesan elector who is a representative of the laity shall vote in the area to which the body by which he was elected belongs, and a diocesan elector who is not a representative of the laity shall vote in such area as the diocesan synod may decide. Any such division shall remain in force until it is revoked by the diocesan synod.

(3) If a diocesan synod decides to divide the diocese into two or more areas in pursuance of this rule the division shall be made in such manner that the number of members to be elected in any such area will be not less than three.

Conduct of Elections

39. (1) Subject to any directions by the General Synod or the Presidents thereof, elections to the House of Laity shall be carried out during the three months immediately following any dissolution of the General Synod and shall be so carried out in each diocese during such period within the said three months as shall be fixed by the archbishops of Canterbury and York.

(2) The presiding officer in each diocese or each area of a diocese shall be the registrar of the diocese or a person appointed by him with the approval of the registrar of the province, except that, if the said registrar is a candidate in the election, the presiding officer shall be a person appointed by the registrar of the province. The expenses of the elections shall be paid out of diocesan funds.

(3) On receipt of the names and addresses of the qualified electors from the diocesan electoral registration officer the presiding officer shall ensure that in respect of the election –

(i) those persons are sent or given nomination papers; and

(ii) only such persons are sent or given voting papers at the address entered against their names in the register of electors.

The presiding officer shall also send nomination papers to any other person who requests them.

(4) Every candidate must be nominated and seconded by diocesan electors qualified to vote in the area in which the candidate is seeking to be elected. All nominations shall be in writing, shall include the year of the candidate's birth and a statement as to whether the candidate is seeking re-election and, if so, as to the dates of the candidate's previous service and shall be delivered either by post, by facsimile transmission or in person to the presiding officer of the area, together with evidence of the candidate's consent to serve, within such period, being a period of not less than twenty-eight days ending on such date as may be specified by the presiding officer, provided that where a nomination paper has been sent by facsimile transmission the name of the candidate shall not appear on the voting paper unless the original nomination paper has been received by the presiding officer within three days of the closing date for nominations.

(5) It shall be the duty of the presiding officer –

(a) to scrutinise nomination papers as soon as they have been lodged and he shall, without delay, inform the candidate concerned whether the nomination is valid. Where the nomination is invalid the presiding officer shall give his reasons for so ruling and if, by the close of the nomination period, no valid nomination is received, the candidate shall be excluded from the election;

(b) to supply free of charge to a duly nominated candidate in the election one copy of the names and addresses of the qualified electors (including, if an elector has authorized the use of an electronic mail address, that address) within seven days of receiving his written request.

(6) If any of the candidates so request the presiding officer shall despatch to every elector election addresses from those candidates being not more than one sheet of A4 paper. One copy of the address shall be provided by the candidates at their own expense and be delivered or sent by electronic mail to the presiding officer by such date as he shall determine being not less than seven days after the close of nominations. The presiding officer shall be under no obligation to despatch to electors election addresses which are received after the due date or which are not in the prescribed form.

(7) It shall be the duty of the presiding officer in any election under these rules to seek to ensure that during the period beginning with the date on which nominations are invited and ending on the last date for the return of voting papers, no papers or other literature except election addresses prepared by the candidates under paragraph (6) of this rule shall be circulated to the electors by him or by or under authority of the diocesan synod or in the deanery synod or distributed at a synod meeting which in his opinion are likely to prejudice the election. The rural dean and the lay chairman and secretary of the deanery synod shall also be under a duty to seek to ensure that during the election period no papers or other literature form part of an official circulation or are distributed at a synod meeting which in the opinion of any of them are likely to prejudice the election.

(8) Subject to rule 51, if more candidates are nominated for any area than there are seats to be filled, the election shall be conducted by voting papers by the method of the single transferable vote under rules to be made from time to time as provided by the Standing Orders of the General Synod. Every voting paper, which shall include the year of birth of each candidate and a statement as to whether the candidate is seeking re-election and, if so, as to the dates of the candidate's previous service, shall be marked and signed on the reverse thereof by the elector and shall be returnable to the presiding officer within such period, being a period of not less than twenty-one days after the date on which the voting paper is issued, as that officer may specify, provided that a voting paper sent by facsimile transmission shall not be counted as a valid vote.

(9) A candidate or a person nominated by him has the right to be present at the counting of the votes in order to scrutinise the count but shall take no part in it. The presiding officer shall give not less than seven days' notice in writing to each candidate of the time and place at which the votes are to be counted.

(10) Where within seven days of a count being completed the presiding officer is of the opinion that a recount should take place because of a possible irregularity or inaccuracy in the count, he may, with the concurrence of the registrar of the province, order such a recount and shall give notice in writing to each candidate of the time and place at which the votes are to be recounted.

(11) A full return of the result of any election and of the result sheet shall be sent by the presiding officer within four working days of the declaration of the result to every candidate in the election, the Clerk to the General Synod and an election scrutineer appointed by the Business Committee of the General Synod. The scrutineer shall have power within ten days of the declaration of the result to order a recount of the voting papers if in his opinion this might be material to the result of the election.

(12) The result sheet shall be publicly displayed in the diocesan office in such manner as the bishop may approve and at the General Synod office until the end of the first group of sessions of the new Synod as the Clerk to the General Synod may direct.

(13) The presiding officer in each area shall ensure that the valid voting papers received by him for the purposes of any election to the House of Laity are preserved for a period of not less than two years beginning with the date of the election.

[Duties and Payment of Presiding Officers]‡

40. (1) Rules defining the duties to be undertaken by the presiding officers in connection with elections to the House of Laity shall be prepared by the provincial registrars acting jointly, but no such rules shall have effect unless approved by the lay members of the Business Committee of the General Synod.

(2) A presiding officer shall be entitled to such fees for the performance by him of the duties aforesaid as may be specified in any order for the time being in force made under the Ecclesiastical Fees Measure 1986; and where with the prior agreement in writing of the bishop's council and standing committee the presiding officer or any other person performs any other duties in connection with elections to the House of Laity he shall be entitled to such fees as may be specified in the agreement.

---

‡ This header does not appear in the statutory text.

Term of office of membership of General Synod and other bodies

41. The term of office of elected members of the House of Laity, of the members elected or chosen under rule 35(1)(d) above and of members chosen by the lay members of religious communities shall be for the lifetime of the General Synod for which they are elected or chosen, but without prejudice to their acting under Article 3(4) of the Constitution[1] during the period of the dissolution of the General Synod or to their continuing to be ex-officio members of other bodies constituted under these rules during that period.

EX-OFFICIO AND CO-OPTED MEMBERS OF THE HOUSE OF LAITY

42. (1) The following persons, if they are not in Holy Orders, shall be ex-officio members of the House of Laity –

(a) the Dean of the Arches and Auditor;

(b) the Vicar-General of the Province of Canterbury;

(c) the Vicar-General of the Province of York;

(d) the three Church Estates Commissioners;

(e) the Chairman of the Central Board of Finance;

(f) the Chairman of the Church of England Pensions Board;

(g) the members of the Archbishops' Council who are actual communicants.

(2) The House of Laity shall have power to co-opt persons who are actual lay communicants of eighteen years or upwards to be members of the House of Laity:
Provided that –

(a) the co-opted members shall not at any time exceed five in number; and

(b) no person shall be qualified to become a co-opted member unless not less than two-thirds of the members of the Standing Committee of the House of Laity shall have first consented to his being co-opted, either at a meeting of the Standing Committee or in writing.

(3) Except in regard to their appointment, the ex-officio and co-opted members shall have the same rights and be subject to the same rules and regulations as elected members: . . . Where such members are on more than

one electoral roll, they shall choose the parochial church council of which they are to be a member.

(4) Co-opted members shall continue to be members of the House of Laity until the next dissolution of the General Synod, but without prejudice to their acting under Article 3(4) of the Constitution[2] during the period of the dissolution or to their continuing to be ex-officio members of other bodies constituted under these rules during that period:

Provided that the House of Laity may, in the case of any co-opted member, fix a shorter period of membership.

(5) The House of Laity may make standing orders for regulating the procedure of and incidental to the appointment of co-opted members and otherwise for carrying this rule into effect.

PART VI
APPEALS AND DISQUALIFICATIONS

[ENROLMENT APPEALS]‡

43. (1) There shall be a right of appeal with regard to –

(a) any enrolment, or refusal of enrolment, on the roll of a parish or the registers of lay or clerical electors;

(b) the removal of any name, or the refusal to remove any name, from the roll of a parish or the registers of lay or clerical electors.

(2) The following persons shall have a right of appeal under this rule –

(a) a person who is refused enrolment on the roll or register;

(b) a person whose name is removed from the roll or register; or

(c) any person whose name is entered on the roll or register who wishes to object to the enrolment or removal of the name of any other person on that roll or register.

(3) In an appeal concerning the roll of a parish, notice of the appeal shall be given in writing to the lay chairman of the deanery synod and in an appeal concerning the register of lay or clerical electors notice of the appeal shall be given in writing to the Chairman of the House of Laity or the Chairman of the House of Clergy of the diocesan synod as the case may be.

(4) Notice of appeal shall be given not later than fourteen days after the date of notification of the enrolment, removal or refusal or not later than fourteen days after the last day of the publication (as provided by rule 2(3)) of a new roll or register or of a list of additions or removals from such roll or register.

(5) In any appeal arising under this rule the chairman of the house concerned of the diocesan synod or the lay chairman of the deanery synod, as the case may be, shall within fourteen days refer any appeal to the bishop's council and standing committee of the diocese unless within that period the

---

‡ Header appears in upper case in error in the statutory text.

appellant withdraws the appeal in writing. The said bishop's council shall appoint three or a greater number being an odd number of their lay members or clerical members as the case may be to consider and decide the appeal.

[ELECTION APPEALS]‡

44. (1) There shall be a right of appeal with regard to –

(a) the allowance or disallowance of any vote given or tendered in an election of a churchwarden or in an election under these rules or to a body constituted under or in accordance with these rules;

(b) the result of any election of a churchwarden or of any election or choice held or made or purporting to be held or made under these rules, or any election or choice of members of a body constituted under or in accordance with these rules.

(2) The following persons shall have a right of appeal under this rule –

(a) an elector in the said election;

(b) a candidate in the said election; or

(c) the chairman of the house of laity or of the house of clergy of the diocesan synod or, in an election to the House of Laity of the General Synod, the Chairman and Vice-Chairman of that House of Laity as specified in paragraph (5) of this rule.

(3) The provisions of this rule (except paragraph (6)), insofar as they confer a right of appeal by any person referred to in paragraph (2) above against the result of an election and provide for notice of an appeal and the determination thereof, shall apply in relation to an election in the House of Laity of the General Synod by the diocesan electors of the diocese in Europe.

(4) Subject to paragraph (6) of this rule in the case of an appeal arising out of an election to the House of Laity of the General Synod or the diocesan synod notice of the appeal shall be given in writing to the chairman of the house of laity of the diocesan synod. In any other case concerning the laity, notice of the appeal shall be given in writing to the lay chairman of the deanery synod. Notices under this paragraph shall be given:

(a) in the case of an appeal against the allowance or disallowance of a vote, not later than fourteen days after such an allowance or disallowance;

---

‡ Header appears in upper case in error in the statutory text.

(b) in the case of an appeal against the result of an election or choice, not later than fourteen days after the day on which the result is declared by the presiding officer.

(5) The Chairman and Vice-Chairman of the House of Laity of the General Synod shall each have a right of appeal under this rule in accordance with paragraph (1) of this rule in respect of any election to the House of Laity of the General Synod in either of the provinces of Canterbury and York and he shall give notice in writing of such appeal to the presiding officer concerned not later than three months after the result of the election has been declared by the said presiding officer. Provided that if the office of Chairman or Vice-Chairman is vacant when the result of the election is published the person who last held office shall be deemed to hold that office for the purposes of this rule.

(6) An error in the electoral roll or the registers of clerical or lay electors shall not be a ground of appeal against the result of any election unless –

(a) either it has been determined under this rule that there has been such an error or the question is awaiting determination under rule 43; and

(b) the error would or might be material to the result of the election;

and the allowance or disallowance of a vote shall not be a ground of appeal against the result of an election unless the allowance or disallowance would or might be material to the result of the election.

(7) An error in the electoral roll of a chaplaincy or in the register of lay electors in the diocese in Europe shall not be a ground of appeal against the result of an election to the House of Laity of the General Synod by the diocesan electors of that diocese unless –

(a) either it has been determined under the rule which applies in that diocese and corresponds with rule 43 that there has been such an error or the question is awaiting determination under that rule; and

(b) the error would or might be material to the result of that election;

and the allowance or disallowance of a vote shall not be a ground of appeal against the result of such an election unless the allowance or disallowance would or might be material to the result of the election.

(8) An appeal arising out of an election or choice of members of the House of Laity of the General Synod shall, within the period of fourteen days of the appeal being lodged, be referred to the Chairman and Vice-Chairman

of that House unless, within that period, the appellant withdraws the appeal in writing. Subject to paragraph (9) of this rule, the Chairman and Vice-Chairman acting jointly shall appoint three persons (one of whom shall be a qualified lawyer) from an appeal panel consisting of the Dean of the Arches and Auditor, the Vicar General of the Province of Canterbury, the Vicar General of the Province of York and twelve members of the House of Laity of the General Synod nominated by the Appointments Committee of the Church of England to consider and decide the appeal.

(9)(a) Where the Chairman or Vice-Chairman of the House of Laity has given notice of appeal under paragraph (5) above, or where he comes from the diocese to which the appeal relates he shall take no part in the appointing of the three persons to hear the appeal and he shall not be appointed to hear the appeal.

(b) Where a member of the appeal panel comes from the diocese to which the appeal relates, or might otherwise have a benefit from the outcome of the election, he shall not be appointed to hear the appeal.

(10) In any appeal arising under this rule except an appeal arising out of an election to the House of Laity of the General Synod, the chairman of the house of laity of the diocesan synod or the lay chairman of the deanery synod, as the case may be, shall refer any appeal to the bishop's council and standing committee of the diocese who shall appoint three or a greater number, being an odd number, of their lay members to consider and decide the appeal.

(11) In any appeal arising under this rule to the house of clergy of the diocesan synod the chairman of the house of clergy of the said synod shall refer any appeal to the bishop's council and standing committee of the diocese who shall appoint three or a greater number, being an odd number, of their clerical members to consider and decide the appeal.

(12) Where an appeal is pending under this rule in respect of an election to any synod any person who was declared elected in accordance with rule [33]‡ but whose election is or may be affected by the appeal shall for all purposes be deemed to be a member of that synod until the appeal is heard and disposed of.

45. For the purpose of the consideration and decision of any appeal under rules 43 and 44, the persons appointed to consider and decide the appeal –

(a) shall consider all the relevant circumstances and shall be entitled to

---

‡ The correct cross-reference should be to Rule 39.

inspect all documents and papers relating to the subject matter of the appeal and be furnished with all information respecting the same which they may require;

(b) shall give to the parties to the appeal an opportunity of appearing before them in person or through a legal or other representative;

(c) shall have power at any time to extend the time within which a notice of appeal is given;

(d) shall, unless by consent of the persons appointed the appeal is withdrawn, determine the matter at issue and, in an election appeal shall determine whether –

> (i) the person or persons whose election is complained of was or were duly elected;
>
> (ii) the facts complained of amount to a minor infringement of the rules which did not affect the outcome of the election in which event the appeal shall be dismissed; or
>
> (iii) the facts complained of amount to a procedural irregularity in the conduct of the election, but that in all the relevant circumstances the appeal shall be dismissed; or
>
> (iv) the election was void. The determination so certified shall be final as to the matters at issue and, in any case in which there has been no valid election, the members shall direct a fresh election to be held and shall give such directions in connection therewith as they may think necessary;

(e) shall have power at any time to consent to the withdrawal of the appeal by an appellant subject to a determination in respect of costs in accordance with paragraph (f) of this rule;

(f) shall have power to direct that any party to an appeal shall be entitled to payment of costs by any other party or by the diocesan board of finance and to direct that a party shall be responsible for the reasonable expenses of the persons appointed to hear the appeal; save that in so far as the same have not been paid by any other person, the diocesan board of finance shall pay all expenses of the persons appointed to hear the appeal provided that the said board shall first be satisfied that they are reasonable in amount.

Vacation of Seat by Member ceasing to be Qualified for Election

46. (1) Where –

(a) any lay member of a deanery synod, being a parochial representative or a representative under rule 27, ceases to be entered on the roll of the parish by which he was elected or, as the case may be, on the community roll of the cathedral church of the diocese or to be declared under the said rule to be an habitual worshipper at the cathedral church;

(b) any member of a diocesan synod elected by the house of clergy of a deanery synod ceases to be qualified for election by that house;

(c) any lay member of a diocesan synod elected by the house of laity of a deanery synod ceases to have the qualification of entry on the roll of any parish in that deanery or (in appropriate cases) of being on the community roll of the cathedral church of the diocese or of being declared an habitual worshipper at the cathedral church of the diocese under rule 27;

(d) any elected member of the House of Laity of the General Synod ceases to have the qualification of entry on the roll of any parish in the diocese for which he was elected or of being, as the case may be, on the community roll of the cathedral church of the diocese or declared an habitual worshipper as aforesaid;

(e) any elected member of the House of Laity of the General Synod takes any paid office or employment as provided by rule 46A(c);

(f) any member of a deanery synod, a diocesan synod or of the House of Laity of the General Synod has his election declared void in accordance with the provision of rule 45 or becomes disqualified in accordance with the provisions of rule 46A(a) hereof[,.]‡

his seat shall subject to the following provisions of this rule forthwith be vacated.

(2) If the name of a person to whom paragraph 1(a) of this rule applies is entered on the roll of any parish in the diocese other than that of the parish referred to in that paragraph or, as the case may be, on the community roll of the cathedral church of the diocese or if he is declared under rule 27 to be an habitual worshipper at the cathedral church of the diocese, his seat shall not

---

‡ A comma and a full stop appear in error in the statutory text.

be vacated under this rule if, before the vacancy occurs, the parochial church council so resolve.

(3) If a person to whom paragraph (1)(b) of this rule applies continues to work or reside in the diocese, his seat shall not be vacated under this rule if, before the vacancy occurs, the clerical members of the standing committee of the deanery synod so resolve.

(4) If the name of a person to whom paragraph (1)(c) of this rule applies is entered on the roll of any parish in the diocese other than that of the parish referred to in that paragraph or, as the case may be, on the community roll of the cathedral church of the diocese or if he is declared under rule 27 to be an habitual worshipper at the cathedral church of the diocese, neither his seat as a member of that House nor his seat as a lay member of the diocesan synod shall be vacated under this rule if, before the vacancy occurs, the lay members of the standing committee of the deanery synod so resolve.

(5) If the lay members of the bishop's council and standing committee [has]‡ determined before the vacancy occurs that a person to whom paragraph (1)(d) of this rule applies is able and willing to continue to discharge to their satisfaction the duties of a member of the House of Laity elected for that diocese, neither his seat as a member of that House nor his seat as a lay member of the diocesan synod shall be vacated under this rule.

(5A) The lay members of the bishop's council and standing committee shall not later than one year after the determination referred to in paragraph (5) above and annually thereafter review the membership of a member to whom paragraph (1)(d) above applies and determine whether he is able and willing as mentioned in paragraph (5) above.

(6) This rule shall apply in relation to a member of the House of Laity of the General Synod elected for the diocese in Europe with the substitution for the words in paragraph (1)(d) from "roll" to "aforesaid" of the words "electoral roll of any chaplaincy in that diocese".

[Disqualification]‡‡

46A. (a) A person shall be disqualified from being nominated, chosen or

---

‡ The statutory text should read 'have'.
‡‡ This header does not appear in the statutory text.

elected or from serving as a churchwarden, a member of a parochial church council, a district church council or any synod under these rules if he is disqualified from being a charity trustee under section 72(1) of the Charities Act 1993[1] and the disqualification is not for the time being subject to a general waiver by the Charity Commissioners under subsection (4) of that section or to a waiver by them under that subsection in respect of all ecclesiastical charities established for purposes relating to the parish concerned.

In this paragraph "ecclesiastical charity" has the same meaning as that assigned to that expression in the Local Government Act 1894;

(b) A person shall also be disqualified from being nominated, chosen or elected or from serving as a churchwarden or member of a parochial church council if he has been so disqualified from holding office under section 10(6) of the Incumbents (Vacation of Benefices) Measure [1997][‡],[2]

(c) A person shall be disqualified from being nominated for election or from continuing to serve as a member of the General Synod if he holds or takes any paid office or employment appointment to which is or may be made or confirmed by the General Synod, the Convocations, the Archbishops' Council, the Central Board of Finance, the Church Commissioners for England (except that such disqualification shall not apply to any Commissioner so appointed in receipt of a salary or other emoluments), the Church of England Pensions Board or the Corporation of the Church House.

Ex-Officio Membership not to Disqualify for Election

47. No ... person shall be disqualified from being elected or chosen a member of any body under these rules by the fact that he is also a member ex-officio of that body; and no ... person shall be deemed to vacate his seat as such an elected or chosen member of any body by reason only of the fact that subsequently to his election or choice he has become a member of that body ex-officio.

---

‡ The reference should be to the Incumbents (Vacation of Benefices) Measure 1977.

PART VII
SUPPLEMENTARY AND INTERPRETATION

Casual Vacancies

48. (1) Casual vacancies among the parochial representatives elected to the parochial church council or deanery synod shall be filled as soon as practicable after the vacancy has occurred. Where the annual parochial church meeting is not due to be held within the next two months following the occurrence of the vacancy, a vacancy among the parochial representatives elected to the parochial church council may be filled, and a vacancy among the parochial representatives elected to the deanery synod shall be filled, by the election by the parochial church council of a person qualified to be so elected. Returns of parochial representatives of the laity elected to fill one or more casual vacancies on the deanery synod shall be sent by the secretary of the parochial church council to the diocesan electoral registration officer and to the secretary of the deanery synod.

(2) Where a casual vacancy among the members of a diocesan synod elected by either house of a deanery synod occurs, the vacancy may be filled by the election by that house of a person qualified to be so elected, and a meeting of the members of that house who are electors may be held for that purpose.

(3) Subject to paragraphs (1), (2) and (6) of this rule, casual vacancies among persons elected under these rules shall be filled and elections to fill such vacancies shall be conducted in the same manner as ordinary elections. The qualifying date for diocesan electors shall be determined in accordance with rule 35(5).

(4) Elections to fill casual vacancies shall, where possible, be held at such times as will enable all casual vacancies among representatives of the laity who are electors to be filled at the time of every election to the House of Laity of the General Synod, but no such election shall be invalid by reason of any casual vacancies not having been so filled.

(5)(a) Subject to the provisions of this rule, an election to fill a casual vacancy in the House of Laity shall be completed, so far as possible, within six months from the occurrence of the vacancy and, in the event of the vacancy not being filled within that period, the chairman of the House of Laity of the General Synod may give directions to the presiding officer as to the date by which the vacancy must be filled.

(b) Where a casual vacancy occurs in the House of Laity of the General Synod and the period for holding a general election to that House is due to begin within twelve months of the vacancy, the vacancy shall not be filled unless the lay members of the bishop's council and standing committee, acting in accordance with any directions of the diocesan synod, otherwise direct.

(c) Where a casual vacancy in the House of Laity of the General Synod occurs within the period of two years –

(i) beginning with the 1st August in the year of the last general election to that House, or

(ii) beginning with the date of the declaration of the result of an election to fill a casual vacancy where the election was conducted by voting papers in the same manner as a general election;

the election to fill the casual vacancy shall be conducted by those papers in accordance with paragraph (6) of this rule.

(6)(a) Where the election is to be conducted by the voting papers of a general election, the number of persons to be elected shall be the same as in the general election, provided that no continuing candidate elected during the original count shall be excluded.

(b) Where the election is to be conducted by the voting papers of an election other than the general election, the number of persons to be elected shall be calculated by adding together the number of persons previously elected using these voting papers who are still continuing as elected persons, and the number of casual vacancies to be filled, provided that no continuing candidate elected during the original count shall be excluded.

(c) The presiding officer for the area in question shall ask every candidate not elected in the previous election who is still qualified for election for the diocese in question if he consents to serve.

(d) If the number of candidates is the same as the places to be filled and he or they so consent or only one of those candidates so consents he shall be elected to fill the casual vacancy.

(e) If more candidates than places to be filled so consent the votes validly cast in the preceding election shall be recounted from the beginning in accordance with the rules mentioned in rule 39(8), the presiding officer having first withdrawn those candidates who do not consent or are no longer eligible for election.

(7) An election to fill a casual vacancy in either house of the diocesan synod shall be completed so far as possible within six months from the occurrence of the vacancy, provided that where a casual vacancy occurs in either house and the period for holding a general election to that house is due to begin within nine months of the vacancy, the vacancy shall not be filled unless the members of the bishop's council and standing committee who are from the same house otherwise direct.

(8) The preceding provisions of this rule shall apply, so far as applicable and with the necessary modifications, to the choosing of persons under these rules as it applies to the election of persons thereunder, and shall also apply to the election or choosing of members of any body constituted under or in accordance with these rules.

(9) Any person elected or chosen to fill a casual vacancy shall hold office only for the unexpired portion of the term of office of the person in whose place he is elected or chosen.

(10) In calculating the period of six months referred to in paragraphs (5) and (7) of this rule –

(a) where during the course of an election irregularities are found which are of such a kind that the presiding officer is of the opinion that he should declare the proceedings null and void, he shall so declare and shall notify all electors of the declaration and shall cause a fresh election to be held which shall be completed within the period of six months from the date of the notice to the electors of the fresh election;

(b) where in an appeal a determination is made that there has been no valid election and the presiding officer is directed to hold a fresh election, the period of six months shall run from the date of such direction.

(11) In this rule the expression 'casual vacancy' includes the case where insufficient candidates have been nominated to fill the places available.

Resignations

49. Any person holding any office under these rules or being a member of any body constituted by or under these rules may resign his office or membership by notice in writing signed by him and sent or given to the secretary of the body of which he is an officer or member, as the case may be; and his resignation shall take effect on the date specified in the notice or, if no date is so specified, on the receipt of the notice by the secretary of that body.

Notices

50. Any notice or other document required or authorised to be sent or given under these rules shall be deemed to have been duly sent or given if sent through the post addressed to the person to whom it is required or authorised to be sent or given at that person's last known address.

Constraints in Elections

51. (1) If in any election conducted in accordance with these rules it is a requirement that a given number or not less than a given number of places of those elected shall be filled by candidates of a named category, the presiding officer shall follow the procedure set out in paragraphs (2) to (4) of this rule.

(2) The presiding officer shall examine the nomination papers to ascertain if the number of candidates nominated in any named category is less than or equal to the required given number.

(3) If the number of candidates nominated in any named category is less than or equal to the required given number, those candidates shall be declared to be elected and their names shall not be included on the voting paper and thereafter the requirement shall be disregarded and the election shall proceed with the number of seats to be filled being reduced by the number of persons declared elected.

(4) The presiding officer shall circulate with the voting papers a separate notice giving the names of any who have been declared elected in accordance with paragraph (3) of this rule.

Revocation and Variation of Rules, etc.

52. Subject to the provisions of these rules any power conferred by these rules to make, approve, frame, pass or adopt any rule, order, resolution, determination, decision, appointment or scheme, or to give any consent or settle any constitution, or to prescribe the manner of doing anything, shall be construed as including a power, exercisable in a like manner and subject to the like conditions, to revoke or vary any such rule, order, resolution, determination, decision, appointment, scheme, consent or constitution, or anything so prescribed.

Special Provisions

53. (1) In the carrying out of these rules in any diocese the bishop of such diocese shall have power –

(a) to make provision for any matter not herein provided for;

(b) to appoint a person to do any act in respect of which there has been any neglect or default on the part of any person or body charged with any duty under these rules;

(c) so far as may be necessary for the purpose of giving effect to the intention of these rules, to extend or alter the time for holding any meeting or election or to modify the procedure laid down by these rules in connection therewith, provided that such power shall not be exercised in relation to the conduct of the elections referred to in rules 39 and 48 of these rules;

(d) subject to paragraph 1(c) of this rule, in any case in which any difficulties arise, to give any directions which he may consider expedient for the purpose of removing the difficulties.

(2) The powers of the bishop under this rule shall not enable him –

(a) to validate anything that was invalid at the time when it was done;

(b) to give any direction that is contrary to any resolution of the General Synod.

(3) No proceedings of any body constituted under these rules shall be invalidated by any vacancy in the membership of that body or by any defect in the qualification, election or appointment of any members thereof.

(4) No proceedings shall be invalidated by the use of a form which differs from that prescribed by these rules if the form which has in fact been used is to a substantially similar effect. Any question as to whether the form which has been used is to a substantially similar effect shall be determined by the bishop.

(5) In the case of an omission in any parish to prepare or maintain a roll or form or maintain a council or to hold the annual meeting, the rural dean

upon such omission being brought to his notice shall ascertain and report to the bishop the cause thereof.

(6) During a vacancy in an archbishopric or where by reason of illness an archbishop is unable to exercise his functions under these rules or to appoint a commissary under paragraph (10) of this rule the functions of an archbishop under these rules shall be exercisable by the other archbishop.

(7) During a vacancy in a diocesan bishopric the functions of a diocesan bishop under these rules, including his functions as president of the diocesan synod, shall be exercisable by such person, being a person in episcopal orders, as the archbishop of the province may appoint.

(8) Where by reason of illness a diocesan bishop is unable to exercise his functions under these rules or to appoint a commissary under paragraph (10) of this rule, the archbishop of the province may, if he thinks it necessary or expedient to do so, appoint a person in episcopal orders to exercise the functions mentioned in paragraph (7) of this rule during the period of the bishop's illness.

(9) If a person appointed in pursuance of paragraph (7) or (8) of this rule becomes unable by reason of illness to act under the appointment, the archbishop may revoke the appointment and make a fresh one.

(10) An archbishop or diocesan bishop may appoint a commissary and delegate to him all or any of the functions of the archbishop or bishop under these rules, but if a bishop proposes to delegate to a commissary his functions as president of the diocesan synod he shall appoint a person in episcopal orders as commissary.

(11) If a person appointed in pursuance of paragraph (7) or (8) of this rule, or a person to whom the functions of a bishop as president of the diocesan synod are delegated under paragraph (10) of this rule, is a member of the house of clergy of the diocesan synod, his membership of that house shall be suspended during the period for which the appointment or delegation has effect.

(12) The preceding provisions of this rule shall have effect in the diocese in Europe as if the references therein to these rules were references to such of these rules as apply in that diocese, and subject to paragraph (6) of this rule, the powers of an archbishop under this rule shall, as respects that diocese, be exercisable by the Archbishop of Canterbury.

Meaning of Minister, Parish and other words and phrases

54. (1) In these rules –

"actual communicant" means a person who has received communion according to the use of the Church of England or of a Church in communion with the Church of England at least three times during the twelve months preceding the date of his election or appointment being a person whose name is on the roll of a parish and is either –

(a) confirmed or ready and desirous of being confirmed; or

(b) receiving the Holy Communion in accordance with the provisions of Canon B 15A paragraph 1(b);

"auditor" shall mean a person eligible as the auditor of a charity under section 43(2) of the Charities Act 1993;[1]

"independent examiner" shall mean a person as defined in section 43(3)(a) of the Charities Act 1993;[2]

"the Measure" means the Synodical Government Measure 1969;

"minister" means –

(a) the incumbent of a parish;

(b) a curate licensed to the charge of a parish or a minister acting as priest-in-charge of a parish in respect of which rights of presentation are suspended; and

(c) a vicar in a team ministry to the extent that the duties of a minister are assigned to him by a pastoral scheme or order or his licence from the bishop;

"parish" means –

(a) an ecclesiastical parish; and

(b) a district which is constituted a "conventional district" for the cure of souls . . .

(c) in relation to the diocese in Europe, a chaplaincy which is constituted as part of the diocese.

[(d) repealed.]

"public worship" means public worship according to the rites and ceremonies of the Church of England.

(2) Any reference in these rules to the laity shall be construed as a reference to persons other than clerks in Holy Orders, and the expression "lay" in these rules shall be construed accordingly.

(3) Where a person has executed a deed of relinquishment under the Clerical Disabilities Act 1870 and the deed has been enrolled in the High Court and recorded in the registry of a diocese under that Act then, unless and until the vacation of the enrolment of the deed is recorded in such a registry under the Clerical Disabilities Act 1870 (Amendment) Measure 1934, that person shall be deemed not to be a clerk in Holy Orders for the purpose of paragraph (2) of this rule or of any other provision of these rules which refers to such a clerk.

(4) References in these rules to the cathedral church of the diocese shall include, in the case of the dioceses of London and Oxford, references to Westminster Abbey and St George's Chapel, Windsor, respectively.

(5) If any question arises ... whether a Church is a ... Church in communion with the Church of England, it shall be conclusively determined for the purposes of these rules by the Archbishops of Canterbury and York.

(6) In these rules words importing residence include residence of a regular nature but do not include residence of a casual nature.

(7) Any reference herein to "these rules" shall be construed as including a reference to the Appendices hereto.

(8)(a) In these rules any matters or regulations[3] to be prescribed shall be prescribed by the Business Committee of the General Synod [of the General Synod]‡ in accordance with the following procedure.

(b) Any matters or regulations made under this rule shall be laid before the General Synod and shall not come into force until they have been approved by the General Synod, whether with or without amendment.

(c) Where the Business Committee of the General Synod determines that matters or regulations made under this rule do not need to be debated by the General Synod then, unless –

    (i) notice is given by a member of the General Synod in accordance with Standing Orders that he wishes the business to be debated, or

    (ii) notice is so given by any such member that he wishes to move an amendment to the business,

the matters or regulations shall for the purposes of sub-paragraph (b) above be deemed to have been approved by the General Synod without amendment.

---

‡ The words in square brackets appear in error in the statutory text.

APPENDIX I

[SYNODICAL GOVERNMENT FORMS]‡

Section 1   [Rule 1(2)]‡‡

APPLICATION FOR ENROLMENT ON THE CHURCH ELECTORAL ROLL OF THE PARISH OF

[   ]

Full Name ....
Full Address ....
Post Code ....

I declare that

1 I am baptised and am aged 16 or over, (or, become 16* on

....)

†2

A I am a member of the Church of England (or of a Church in communion with the Church of England) and am resident in the parish. ☐

OR

B I am a member of the Church of England (or of a Church in communion with the Church of England) and, not being resident in the parish, I have habitually attended public worship in the parish during the period of six months prior to enrolment. ☐

OR

C I am a member in good standing of a Church (not in communion with the Church of England) which subscribes to the doctrine of the Holy Trinity and also declare myself to be a member of the Church of England and I have habitually attended public worship in the parish during the period of six months prior to enrolment. ☐

---

‡ This header does not appear in the statutory text.
‡‡ This reference does not appear in the statutory text.

Appendix I

I declare that the above answers are true and I apply for inclusion on the Church Electoral Roll of the parish.

Signed .... Date ....

* Those who become 16 during the next 12 months may complete the form, and become eligible to be entered on the Roll on their sixteenth birthday.
† Tick one only of boxes 2A, B or C.

Notes

1. The only Churches at present in communion with the Church of England are other Anglican Churches and certain foreign Churches.

2. Membership of the electoral roll is also open to members in good standing of a Church not in communion with the Church of England which subscribes to the doctrine of the Holy Trinity where those members are also prepared to declare themselves to be members of the Church of England.

3. Every six years a new roll is prepared and those on the previous roll are informed so that they can re-apply. If you are not resident in the parish but were on the roll as an habitual worshipper and have been prevented by sickness or absence or other essential reason from worshipping for the past six months, you may write "would" before "have habitually attended" on the form and add "but was prevented from doing so because ... " and then state the reason.

4. If you have any problems over this form, please approach the clergy or lay people responsible for the parish, who will be pleased to help you.

5. In this form "parish" means ecclesiastical parish.

[Synodical Government Forms]

Section 2   Rule 2(1)
FORM OF NOTICE OF REVISION OF CHURCH ELECTORAL ROLL

Diocese of ....
Parish of ....

*Note – The Revision must be completed not less than 15 days or more than 28 days before the Annual Parochial Church Meeting.

Notice is hereby given that the Church Electoral Roll of the above parish will be revised by the Parochial Church Council,* beginning on .... the .... day of .... 19‡ .... and ending on ...., the .... day of .... 19 ....

After such Revision, a copy of the Roll will forthwith be exhibited for not less than 14 days on, or near to, the principal door of the Parish Church for inspection.

Under the Church Representation Rules any persons are entitled to have their names entered on the roll, if they –

(i) are baptised and aged 16 or over;

(ii) have signed a form of application for enrolment;

and either

(iii) are members of the Church of England or of any Church in communion with the Church of England being resident in the parish or (not being resident in the parish) having habitually attended public worship in the parish during the six months prior to the application for enrolment;

or;

(iv) are members in good standing of a Church (not in communion with the Church of England) which subscribes to the doctrine of the Holy Trinity declaring themselves to be also members of the Church of England and having habitually attended public worship in the parish during the period of six months prior to enrolment.

[*proviso repealed.*]

Forms of application for enrolment can be obtained from the undersigned. In order to be entitled to attend the annual parochial church meeting and to take part in its proceedings, forms of application for enrolment must be returned by the date shown above for the ending of the revision of the Church Electoral Roll by the Parochial Church Council. Any error discovered in the roll should at once be reported to the undersigned.

* Note – Not less than 14 days notice must be given.

Dated this* .... day of .... 19 ....

....
                                                               Church Electoral Roll Officer

Address ....

In this Notice "parish" means an ecclesiastical parish.

---

‡ The statutory text refers to "19 ...." throughout Appendix I.

Appendix I

Section 3   Rule 2(4)

FORM OF NOTICE OF PREPARATION OF NEW ROLL

Diocese of ....

Parish of ....

*Note –
The new roll must be completed not less than 15 days or more than 28 days before the Annual Parochial Church Meeting.

Notice is hereby given that under the Church Representation Rules a new Church Electoral Roll is being prepared. All persons who wish to have their names entered on the new Roll[*]‡, whether their names are entered on the present Roll or not, are requested to apply for enrolment ... not later than ....

The new Roll will come into operation on ....

....

The new Roll shall be published for not less than 14 days. Forms of application for enrolment can be obtained from the undersigned. In order to be entitled to attend the annual parochial church meeting and to take part in its proceedings, forms of application for enrolment must be returned by the earlier of the dates given above.

Under the Church Representation Rules any persons are entitled to have their names entered on the Roll, if they –

(i) are baptized and aged 16 or over;

(ii) have signed a form of application for enrolment;

and either

(iii) are members of the Church of England or of any Church in communion with the Church of England being resident in the parish or (not being resident in the parish) having habitually attended public worship in the parish during the six months prior to the application for enrolment;

or;

(iv) are members in good standing of a Church (not in communion with the Church of England) which subscribes to the doctrine of the Holy Trinity declaring themselves to be also members of the Church of England and having habitually attended public worship in the parish during the period of six months prior to enrolment.

Any error discovered in the Roll should at once be reported to the undersigned.

Dated this .... day of .... 19 ....

....

                                                                                   Church Electoral Roll Officer

Address ....

In this Notice "parish" means an ecclesiastical parish.

---

‡ This asterisk does not appear in the statutory text.

Section 4   **Rule [6(1)]**‡

NOTICE OF ANNUAL PAROCHIAL CHURCH MEETING

Parish of ....

The Annual Parochial Church Meeting will be held in ....

....

on .... day of .... at ....

For the election of Parochial representatives of the laity as follows: –

To the Parochial Church Council .... representatives.

*To the Deanery Synod .... representatives.

For the appointment of Sidesmen and the Independent Examiner or Auditor.

For the consideration of:

(a) A Report on changes in the roll since the last annual parochial church meeting;

(b) [an]‡‡ Annual Report on the proceedings of the parochial church council and the activities of the parish generally;

(c) The Financial Statements of the Council for the year ending on the 31st December immediately preceding the meeting audited or independently examined;

(d) A Report upon the fabric, goods and ornaments of the church or churches of the parish;

(e) A Report on the proceedings of the Deanery Synod;

and other matters of parochial or general Church interest.

Notes

1. All persons whose names are entered upon the Church Electoral Roll of the parish (and such persons only) are entitled to vote at the election of parochial representatives of the laity.

2. Subject to the provisions of rule [12(2)](c)‡‡‡, a person is qualified to be elected a parochial representative of the laity if –

---

‡ The reference should be to Rule 7(1).
‡‡ The word 'an' in lower case appears in error in the statutory text.
‡‡‡ The reference should be to rule 14(3)(c).

Appendix I

(a) his name is entered on the church electoral roll of the parish and, unless he is under the age of eighteen years at the date of the election, has been so entered for at least the preceding period of six months;

(b) he is an actual communicant which means that he has received Communion according to the use of the Church of England or of a Church in communion with the Church of England at least three times during the twelve months preceding the date of the election; and

(c) he is of sixteen years or upwards;

(d) he is not disqualified as referred to in paragraph 3 of these Notes.

3. (a) A person shall be disqualified from being nominated, chosen or elected from serving as a churchwarden, a member of a parochial church council, a district church council or any synod under these rules if he is disqualified from being a charity trustee under section 72(1) of the Charities Act 1993 and the disqualification is not for the time being subject to a general waiver by the Charity Commissioners under subsection (4) of that section or to a waiver by them under that subsection in respect of all ecclesiastical charities established for purposes relating to the parish concerned.

In this paragraph "ecclesiastical charity" has the same meaning as that assigned to that expression in the Local Government Act 1894;

(b) A person shall also be disqualified from being nominated, chosen or elected from serving as a churchwarden or member of a parochial church council if he has been so disqualified from holding office under section 10(6) of [the Incumbent (Vacation of Benefice) Measure 1997].‡

4. Any person whose name is on the electoral roll may be appointed as a sidesman.

5. **A scheme is in operation in this parish which provides that any person entitled to vote in the elections of parochial representatives of the laity to the parochial church council or to the deanery synod or to both that council and that synod may make application on the appropriate form to the undersigned for a postal vote. The completed form must be received before the commencement of the Annual Parochial Church Meeting.

** This paragraph should be deleted if no resolution for postal voting is in operation in the parish.

Signed ....

**Minister of the parish

* Include where applicable.

** Or "Vice-Chairman of the Parochial Church Council" as the case may be (see rule [6(3)]‡‡ of the Church Representation Rules).

In this Notice "parish" means an ecclesiastical parish.

---

‡ The reference should be to the Incumbents (Vacation of Benefices) Measure 1977.
‡‡ The reference should be to rule 7(3).

[Synodical Government Forms]

Section 4A **Rule 12(2)**

APPLICATION FOR POSTAL VOTE

Parish of ....

I (Full Christian name and surname) ....

of (Full postal address) ....

....

declare that my name is entered on the church electoral roll of the above parish and I hereby make application for a postal vote in any elections to which postal voting applies to be held at the forthcoming annual parochial church meeting for the parish. The voting paper should be sent or delivered to me at the above address OR* at the following address

....

Dated .... 19 ....

Signed ....

* delete as appropriate.

Appendix I

Section 5 **Rule [26(3)]‡**

NOTICE OF ELECTION TO HOUSE OF CLERGY OR
HOUSE OF LAITY OF DIOCESAN SYNOD

Diocese of ....

Deanery of ....

1. An election of .... members of the House of Clergy/Laity of the Diocesan Synod will be held in the above Deanery on ....

2. Candidates must be nominated and seconded by qualified electors on forms to be obtained from ....

All members, other than co-opted members . . . of the House of Clergy/Laity of the deanery synod are qualified electors.

3. The election will be decided by simple majority/the single transferable vote.

4. Nominations must be received by no later than 12 o'clock (noon) on

....

Date ....

....
Presiding Officer.

---

‡ The reference should be to Rule 32(4).

[Synodical Government Forms]

Section 6   Rule [26(3)]†

FORM OF NOMINATION TO THE HOUSE OF CLERGY OR
HOUSE OF LAITY OF THE DIOCESAN SYNOD

Diocese of ....

Deanery of ....

Election of members of the House of Clergy/Laity of
the Diocesan Synod

We the undersigned, being qualified electors, hereby nominate the following person as a candidate at the election in the above Deanery.

Surname	Christian Names	Address	Year for Birth

Proposer's signature ....

Proposer's full name ....

Address ....

Seconder's signature ....

Seconder's full name ....

Address ....

I, the above named .... hereby declare that I am not subject to any disqualification referred to in the Notes on this form and signify my willingness to serve as a member of the House of Clergy/Laity of the Diocesan Synod if elected.

Candidate's signature ....

Note: This nomination must be sent to ....

       so as to be received no later than 12 noon on ....

All members, other than co-opted members . . . , of the House of Clergy/Laity of the deanery synod are qualified electors.

---

‡ The reference should be to Rule 32(4).

Appendix I

Disqualifications from being nominated (rule 46A)

A person is disqualified from being nominated for membership of any Synod if he is disqualified from being a charity trustee under section 72(1) of the Charities Act 1993 and the disqualification is not for the time being subject to a general waiver by the Charity Commissioners under subsection (4) of that section or to a waiver by them under that subsection in respect of all ecclesiastical charities established for purposes relating to the parish concerned.

In this paragraph "ecclesiastical charity" has the same meaning as that assigned to that expression in the Local Government Act 1894.

[Synodical Government Forms]

Section 7   Rule [26(4)]†

FORM OF VOTING PAPER FOR ELECTIONS TO THE HOUSE OF CLERGY OR THE HOUSE OF LAITY OF THE DIOCESAN SYNOD

.... Diocesan Synod

Election of members of the House of Clergy/Laity

Deanery of ....

.... members to be elected.

Voting Paper

Mark your vote in this column	Candidates' names, addresses . . . and year of birth

Guidance to Voters

1. This voting paper must be signed and the full name written on the reverse.

2. You have as many votes as there are members to be elected.

3. You may not give more than one vote to any one candidate.

4. You vote by placing an 'X' opposite the name(s) of the candidate(s) of your choice.

5. If you inadvertently spoil your voting paper you may return it to the Presiding Officer who will give you another paper.

6. This voting paper duly completed on the reverse thereof must be delivered (by post or otherwise) to ....
so as to arrive by no later than ....

(To be printed on back of form)   Signature of Voter ....

                     Full name ....

                     Address ....

                     ....

‡ The reference should be to Rule 32(6).

Appendix I

Section 8   Rule [26(4)]‡

FORM OF VOTING PAPER FOR ELECTION TO THE HOUSE OF CLERGY OR THE HOUSE OF LAITY OF THE DIOCESAN SYNOD

.... Diocesan Synod

Election of members of the House of Clergy/Laity

Deanery of ....

.... members to be elected.

Voting Paper

Mark your vote in this column	Candidates' names, addresses ... and year of birth

Guidance to Voters

1. This voting paper must be signed and the full name written on the reverse.

2. Use your single transferable vote by entering "1" against your first preference, and if desired, "2" against your second preference, "3" against your third preference, and so on as far as you wish. The sequence of your preferences is crucial. NO CROSS should be used.

3. You should continue to express preferences for as long as you are able to place successive candidates in order. A later preference is considered only if an earlier preference either has a surplus above the quota (the minimum number required to guarantee election) or has been excluded because of insufficient support.

4. The numbering of your preferences must be consecutive and given to different candidates. Remember that your marking a second or subsequent preference cannot affect the chances of any earlier preference.

5. If you inadvertently spoil your voting paper you may return it to the Presiding Officer who will give you another paper.

6. This voting paper duly completed on the reverse thereof must be delivered (by post or otherwise) to .... so as to arrive by no later than ....

            Signature of Voter ....

            Full name ....

            Address ....

            ....

            (To be printed on back of form)

‡ The reference should be to Rule 32(6).

APPENDIX II

Rule [13]†

GENERAL PROVISIONS RELATING TO PAROCHIAL CHURCH COUNCILS

1. (a) The minister of the parish shall be chairman of the parochial church council (hereinafter referred to as "the council"). *Officers of the council*

    (b) A lay member of the council shall be elected as vice-chairman of the council.

    (c) During the vacancy of the benefice or when the chairman is incapacitated by absence or illness or any other cause or when the minister invites him to do so the vice-chairman of the council shall act as chairman and have all the powers vested in the chairman.

    (d) (i) The Council may appoint one of their number to act as secretary of the Council. Failing such appointment the office of secretary shall be discharged by some other fit person who shall not thereby become a member of the council, provided that such person may be co-opted to the Council in accordance with the provisions of rule 14(1)(h);

    (ii) where a person other than a member of the Council is appointed to act as secretary, that person may be paid such remuneration (if any) as the council deems appropriate provided that such person shall not be eligible to be a member of the council;

    (iii) [The]‡‡ secretary shall have charge of all documents relating to the current business of the council except that, unless he is the electoral roll officer, he shall not have charge of the roll. He shall be responsible for keeping the minutes, shall record all resolutions passed by the council and shall keep the secretary of the diocesan synod and deanery synod informed as to his name and address.

    (e) (i) The council may appoint one or more of their number to act as treasurer solely or jointly. Failing such appointment, the office of treasurer shall be discharged either –

    by such of the churchwardens as are members of the council or, if there is only one such churchwarden, by that churchwarden solely; or

    by some other fit person who shall not thereby become a member of the council, provided that such person may be co-opted to the council in accordance with the provisions of rule 14(1)(h).

---

† The reference should be to Rule 15.
‡‡ The text should be 'the'.

Appendix II

    (ii) Where a person other than a member of the Council is appointed to act as treasurer that person may be paid such remuneration (if any) as the Council deems appropriate provided that such person shall not be eligible to be a member of the Council.

(f) The council shall appoint an electoral roll officer, who may but need not be a member of the council and may be the secretary, and if he is not a member may pay to him such remuneration as it shall think fit. He shall have charge of the roll.

(g) If an independent examiner or auditor to the council is not appointed by the annual meeting or if an independent examiner or auditor appointed by the annual meeting is unable or unwilling to act, an independent examiner or auditor (who shall not be a member of the council) shall be appointed by the council for a term of office ending at the close of the next annual meeting. The remuneration (if any) of the independent examiner or auditor shall be paid by the council.

(h) For the purposes of this paragraph, where a special cure of souls in respect of a parish has been assigned to a vicar in a team ministry, or where there has been no such assignment but a special responsibility for pastoral care in respect of the parish has been assigned to a member of the team under section 20(8A) of the Pastoral Measure 1983, that vicar or that member, as the case may be, shall be deemed to be the minister unless incapacitated by absence or illness or any other cause, in which case the rector in the team ministry shall be deemed to be the minister.

Meetings of Council   2. The council shall hold not less than four meetings in each year. Meetings shall be convened by the chairman and if not more than four meetings are held they shall be at quarterly intervals so far as possible.

Power to call meetings   3. The chairman may at any time convene a meeting of the council. If he refuse or neglect to do so within seven days after a requisition for that purpose signed by not less than one-third of the members of the council has been presented to him those members may forthwith convene a meeting.

Notices relating to meetings   4. (a) Except as provided in paragraph 8 of this Appendix, at least ten clear days before any meeting of the council notice thereof specifying the time and place of the intended meeting and signed by or on behalf of the chairman of the council or the persons convening the meeting shall be posted at or near the principal door of every church, or building licensed for public worship in the parish.

(b) Not less than seven days before the meeting a notice thereof specifying the time and place of the meeting signed by or on behalf of the secretary shall be posted or delivered to every member of the council or, if the member has authorized the use of an electronic mail address, to that address. Such notice shall contain the agenda of the meeting including any motion or other business proposed by any member of the council of which notice has been received by the secretary. The notice required by this sub-paragraph shall not be required for a council meeting immediately following the annual parochial church meeting being a council meeting which has been called solely for the purpose of appointing or electing any officers of the council or the members of the standing committee thereof provided that the notice required by sub-paragraph (a) hereof has been given.

(c) If for some good and sufficient reason the chairman, vice-chairman and secretary, or any two of them, consider that a convened meeting should be postponed, notice shall be given to every member of the council specifying a reconvened time and place within fourteen days of the postponed meeting.

- Subject to the provisions of rules 22 and 23 the chair at a meeting of the council shall be taken – {Chairman at meetings}

    (a) by the chairman of the council if he is present;

    (b) if the chairman is not present, by a clerk in Holy Orders, licensed to or with permission to officiate in the parish duly authorized by the bishop with the clerk's agreement, following a joint application by the minister of the parish and the council or, if the benefice is vacant, by the council for the purposes of this sub-paragraph;

    (c) if neither the chairman of the council nor the clerk mentioned in sub-paragraph (b) above is present, by the vice-chairman of the council:

    Provided that at any such meeting the chairman presiding shall, if he thinks it expedient to do so or the meeting so resolves, vacate the chair either generally or for the purposes of any business in which he has a personal interest or for any other particular business.

    Should none of the persons mentioned above be available to take the chair for any meeting or for any particular item on the agenda during a meeting then a chairman shall be chosen by those members present from among their number and the person so chosen shall preside for that meeting or for that particular item.

- No business shall be transacted at any meeting of the council unless at least one-third of the members are present thereat and no business which is not specified in the agenda shall be transacted at any meeting except by the consent of three-quarters of the members present at the meeting. {Quorum and agenda}

- The business of a meeting of the council shall be transacted in the order set forth in the agenda unless the council by resolution otherwise determine. {Order of business}

- In the case of sudden emergency or other special circumstances requiring immediate action by the council a meeting may be convened by the chairman of the council at not less than three clear days' notice in writing to the members of the council but the quorum for the transaction of any business at such meetings shall be a majority of the then existing members of the council and no business shall be transacted at such meeting except as is specified in the notice convening the meeting. {Short Notice for emergency meetings}

Appendix II

Place of meetings	9. The meeting of the council shall be held at such place as the council may direct or in the absence of such direction as the chairman may direct.
Vote of majority to decide	10. The business of the council shall be decided by a majority of the members present and voting thereon.
Casting vote	11. In the case of an equal division of votes the chairman of the meeting shall have a second or casting vote.
Minutes	12. (a) The names of the members present at any meeting of the council shall be recorded in the minutes.

(b) If one-fifth of the members present and voting on any resolution so require, the minutes shall record the names of the members voting for and against that resolution.

(c) Any member of the council shall be entitled to require that the minutes shall contain a record of the manner in which his vote was cast on any resolution.

(d) Minutes of meetings of the council shall be available to all members of the Council. The members shall also have access to past minutes which the Chairman and Vice-Chairman jointly determine to be relevant to current Council business.

(e) The independent examiner or auditor of the Council's financial statements, the bishop, the archdeacon and any person authorised by one of them in writing shall have access to the approved minutes of council meetings without the authority of the Council.

(f) Other persons whose names are on the church electoral roll may have access to the approved minutes of Council meetings held after the annual parochial church meeting in 1995 except any minutes deemed by the Council to be confidential.

(g) Other persons may have access to the minutes of Council meetings only in accordance with a specific authorization of the Council provided that, where minutes have been deposited in the diocesan record office pursuant to the Parochial Registers and Records Measure 1978, the authorization of the council may be dispensed with.

Adjournments	13. Any meeting of the council may adjourn its proceedings to such time and place as may be determined at such meeting.
Standing committee	14. (a) The council shall have a standing committee consisting of not less than five persons. The minister and such of the churchwardens as are members of the council shall be ex-officio members of the standing committee, and the council shall by resolution appoint at least two other members of the standing committee from among its own members and may remove any person so appointed. Unless removed from office, the appointed members shall hold office from the date of their appointment until the conclusion of the next annual meeting of the parish.

(b) The standing committee shall have power to transact the business of the council between the meetings thereof subject to any directions given by the council.

15. The council may appoint other committees for the purpose of the various branches of church work in the parish and may include therein persons who are not members of the council. The minister shall be a member of all committees ex-officio. *Other committees*

16. An independent examiner or auditor of the Council's financial statements shall – *[Independent examiner or auditor]‡*

    (a) have a right of access with respect to books, documents or other records (however kept) which relate to the said financial statements;

    (b) have a right to require information and explanations from past or present treasurers or members of the council and, in case of default, the independent examiner or auditor may apply to the Charity Commissioners for an order for directions pursuant to section 44(2) of the Charities Act 1993[1] or any statutory modification thereof for the time being in force.

17. No proceedings of the council shall be invalidated by any vacancy in the membership of the council or by any defect in the qualification or election of any member thereof. *Validity of proceedings*

18. Any question arising on the interpretation of this Appendix shall be referred to the bishop of the diocese and any decision given by him or by any person appointed by him on his behalf shall be final. *Interpretation*

This side note does not appear in the statutory text.

SUPPLEMENTARY MATERIAL (not forming part of the Rules)

TEXTS OF SELECTED ENACTMENTS REFERRED TO IN THE RULES

Incumbents (Vacation of Benefices) Measures 1977 and 1993
(see Rule 46A)

Section 10 (Powers of Bishop where there has been a pastoral breakdown between incumbent and parishioners)

5. Where the tribunal reports to the bishop that in its opinion the serious breakdown of the pastoral relationship between the incumbent concerned and the parishioners is one to which the conduct of the incumbent concerned has contributed over a substantial period, the bishop may rebuke the incumbent and may, if he thinks fit, disqualify him from executing or performing without the consent of the bishop any such right or duty of or incidental to his office, and during such period, as the bishop may specify.

6. Where the tribunal reports to the bishop that in its opinion such a breakdown as is mentioned in subsection 5 above is one to which the conduct of the parishioners has contributed over a substantial period, the bishop may rebuke such of them as he thinks fit and may, if he thinks fit, disqualify such of them as he thinks fit from being a churchwarden or member or officer of the parochial church council of the parish in question and of such other parishes in his diocese as he may specify during such period not exceeding five years as he may specify.

Charities Act 1993

Section 72 (Persons disqualified for being trustees of a charity) (see Rule 46A)

1. Subject to the following provisions of this section, a person shall be disqualified for being a charity trustee or trustee for a charity if –

   (a) he has been convicted of any offence involving dishonesty or deception;

   (b) he has been adjudged bankrupt or sequestration of his estate has been awarded and (in either case) he has not been discharged;

   (c) he has made a composition or arrangement with, or granted a trust deed for, his creditors and has not been discharged in respect of it;

   (d) he has been removed from the office of charity trustee or trustee for a charity by an order made –

      (i) by the Commissioners under section 18(2)(i) above, or

      (ii) by the Commissioners under section 20(1A)(i) of the Charities Act 1960 (power to act for protection of charities) or under section 20(1)(i) of that Act (as in force before the commencement of section 8 of the Charities Act 1992), or

(iii) by the High Court, on the grounds of any misconduct or mismanagement in the administration of the charity for which he was responsible or to which he was privy, or which he by his conduct contributed to or facilitated;

(e) he has been removed, under section 7 of the Law Reform (Miscellaneous Provisions) (Scotland) Act 1990 (powers of Court of Session to deal with management of charities), from being concerned in the management of control of any body;

(f) he is subject to a disqualification order under the Company Directors Disqualification Act 1986 or to an order made under section 429(2)(b) of the Insolvency Act 1986 (failure to pay under county court administration order).

2. In subsection 1 above –

(a) paragraph (a) applies whether the conviction occurred before or after the commencement of that subsection, but does not apply in relation to any conviction which is a spent conviction for the purposes of the Rehabilitation of Offenders Act 1974;

(b) paragraph (b) applies whether the adjudication of bankruptcy or the sequestration occurred before or after the commencement of that subsection;

(c) paragraph (c) applies whether the composition or arrangement was made, or the trust deed was granted, before or after the commencement of that subsection; and

(d) paragraphs (d) to (f) apply in relation to orders made and removals effected before or after the commencement of that subsection.

3. Where (apart from this subsection) a person is disqualified under subsection 1(b) above for being a charity trustee or trustee for any charity which is a company, he shall not be so disqualified if leave has been granted under section 11 of the Company Directors Disqualification Act 1986 (undischarged bankrupts) for him to act as director of the charity; and similarly a person shall not be disqualified under subsection 1(f) above for being a charity trustee or trustee for such a charity if –

(a) in the case of a person subject to a disqualification order, leave under the order has been granted for him to act as director of the charity, or

(b) in the case of a person subject to an order under section 429(2)(b) of the Insolvency Act 1986, leave has been granted by the court which made the order for him so to act.

4. The Commissioners may, on the application of any person disqualified under subsection 1 above, waive his disqualification either generally or in relation to a particular charity or a particular class of charities; but no such waiver may be granted in relation to any charity which is a company if –

(a) the person concerned is for the time being prohibited, by virtue of –

(i) a disqualification order under the Company Directors Disqualification Act 1986, or

(ii) section 11(1) or 12(2) of that Act (undischarged

Supplementary Material

bankrupts; failure to pay under county court administration order), from acting as director of the charity; and

(b) leave has not been granted for him to act as director of any other company.

5. Any waiver under subsection 4 above shall be notified in writing to the person concerned.

6. For the purposes of this section the Commissioners shall keep, in such manner as they think fit, a register of all persons who have been removed from office as mentioned in subsection 1(d) above either –

(a) by an order of the Commissioners made before or after the commencement of subsection 1 above, or

(b) by an order of the High Court made after the commencement of section 45(1) of the Charities Act 1992;

and, where any person is so removed from office by an order of the High Court, the court shall notify the Commissioners of his removal.

7. The entries in the register kept under subsection 6 above shall be available for public inspection in legible form at all reasonable times.

Churchwardens Measure 2001

Sections 4 Time and manner of choosing and 5 Meeting of the parishioners

Section 4   Time and manner of choosing

1. The churchwardens of a parish shall be chosen annually not later than the 30th April in each year.

2. Subject to the provisions of this Measure the churchwardens of a parish shall be elected by a meeting of the parishioners.

3. Candidates for election at the meeting must be nominated and seconded in writing by persons entitled to attend the meeting and each nomination paper must include a statement, signed by the person nominated, to the effect that that person is willing to serve as a churchwarden and is not disqualified under section 2(1), (2) or (3) above.

4. A nomination shall not be valid unless –

(a) the nomination paper is received by the minister of the parish before the commencement of the meeting; and

(b) in the case of a person who is not qualified by virtue of section 1(3) (a), (b) or (c) above, the bishop's permission was given under section 1(4) above before the nomination paper is received by the minister of the parish.

5. If it appears to the minister of the parish that the election of any particular person nominated might give rise to serious difficulties between the minister and that person in the carrying out of their respective functions the minister may, before the election is conducted, make a statement to the effect that only one churchwarden is to be elected by the meeting. In that event one churchwarden shall be appointed by the minister from among the persons nominated, the name of the person so appointed being

announced before the election is conducted, and the other shall then be elected by the meeting.

6. During any period when there is no minister –

(a) subsection (4) above shall apply with the substitution for the words 'minister of the parish' of the words 'churchwarden by whom the notice convening the meeting was signed'; and

(b) subsection (5) above shall not apply.

7. A person may be chosen to fill a casual vacancy among the churchwardens at any time.

8. Any person chosen to fill a casual vacancy shall be chosen in the same manner as was the churchwarden whose place he is to fill except that, where the churchwarden concerned was appointed by the minister and the minister has ceased to hold office, the new churchwarden to fill the casual vacancy shall be elected by a meeting of the parishioners.

Section 5   Meeting of the parishioners

1. A joint meeting of –

(a) the persons whose names are entered on the church electoral roll of the parish; and

(b) the persons resident in the parish whose names are entered on a register of local government electors by reason of such residence,

shall be deemed to be a meeting of the parishioners for the purposes of this Measure.

2. The meeting of the parishioners shall be convened by the minister or, during any period when there is no minister or when the minister is unable or unwilling to do so, the churchwardens of the parish by a notice signed by the minister or a churchwarden as the case may be.

3. The notice shall state the place, day and hour at which the meeting of the parishioners is to be held.

4. The notice shall be affixed on or near to the principal door of the parish church and of every other building licensed for public worship in the parish for a period including the last two Sundays before the meeting.

5. The minister, if present, or, if he is not present, a chairman chosen by the meeting of the parishioners, shall preside thereat.

6. In case of an equal division of votes on any question other than one to determine an election of a churchwarden the chairman of the meeting of parishioners shall not have a second or casting vote and the motion on that question shall be treated as lost.

7. The meeting of the parishioners shall have power to adjourn, and to determine its own rules of procedure.

8. A person appointed by the meeting of the parishioners shall act as clerk of the meeting and shall record the minutes thereof.

Synodical Government Measure 1969

Article 8 (from Schedule 2 to the Measure) (see Rule 34(1)(e) and (h))

1. A Measure or Canon providing for permanent changes in the Services of

Baptism or Holy Communion or in the Ordinal, or a scheme for a constitutional union or a permanent and substantial change of relationship between the Church of England and another Christian body being a body a substantial number of whose members reside in Great Britain, shall not be finally approved by the General Synod unless, at a stage determined by the Archbishops, the Measure or Canon or scheme, or the substance of the proposals embodied therein, has been approved by a majority of the dioceses at meetings of their diocesan synods or, in the case of the diocese in Europe, of the bishop's council and standing committee of that diocese.

1A. If the Archbishops consider that this Article should apply to a scheme which affects the Church of England and another Christian body but does not fall within paragraph 1 of this Article, they may direct that this Article shall apply to that scheme, and where such a direction is given this Article shall apply accordingly.

1B. The General Synod may by resolution provide that final approval of any such scheme as aforesaid, being a scheme specified in the resolution, shall require the assent of such special majorities of the members present and voting as may be specified in the resolution, and the resolution may specify a special majority of each House or of the whole Synod or of both, and in the latter case the majorities may be different.

1C. A motion for the final approval of a Measure providing for permanent changes in any such Service or in the Ordinal shall not be deemed to be carried unless it receives the assent of a majority in each House of the General Synod of not less than two-thirds of those present and voting.

Section 4(4) (see Rule 34(1)(k))

4. Except as may be provided by standing orders or directions of the diocesan synod, the advisory and consultative functions of the synod under subsections 2(b) and 3 of this section may be discharged on behalf of the synod by the bishop's council and standing committee appointed in accordance with rule 34 of the Church Representation Rules contained in Schedule 3 to this Measure, but either the bishop or the body so appointed may require any matter to be referred to the synod.

Article 3(4) (from Schedule 2 of the Measure) (see Rules 41 and 42(4))

4. A member of the General Synod may continue to act during the period of the dissolution as a member of any such Board, Commission, Committee or body:

Provided that, if a member of the Synod who is elected proctor of the clergy or an elected member of the House of Laity does not stand for re-election or is not re-elected, this paragraph shall cease to apply to him with effect from the date on which the election of his successor is announced by the presiding officer.

Charities Act 1993

Sections 43 (Annual audit or examination of charity accounts) and

44 (Supplementary provisions relating to audits, etc.)

Section 43 (Annual audit or examination of charity accounts) (see Rule 54(1))

1. Subsection 2 below applies to a financial year of a charity ('the relevant year') if the charity's gross income or total expenditure in any of the following, namely –

(a) the relevant year;

(b) the financial year of the charity immediately preceding the relevant year (if any), and

(c) the financial year of the charity immediately preceding the year specified in paragraph (b) above (if any), exceeds £250,000.

2. If this subsection applies to a financial year of a charity, the accounts of the charity for that year shall be audited by a person who –

(a) is, in accordance with section 25 of the Companies Act 1989 (eligibility for appointment), eligible for appointment as a company auditor, or

(b) is a member of a body for the time being specified in regulations under section 44 below and is under the rules of that body eligible for appointment as auditor of the charity.

3. If subsection 2 above does not apply to a financial year of a charity and its gross income or total expenditure in that year exceeds £10,000, then (subject to subsection 4 below) the accounts of the charity for that year shall, at the election of the charity trustees, either –

(a) be examined by an independent examiner, that is to say an independent person who is reasonably believed by the trustees to have the requisite ability and practical experience to carry out a competent examination of the accounts, or

(b) be audited by such a person as is mentioned in subsection 2 above.

4. Where it appears to the Commissioners –

(a) that subsection 2, or (as the case may be) subsection 3 above, has not been complied with in relation to a financial year of a charity within ten months from the end of that year, or

(b) that, although subsection 2 above does not apply to a financial year of a charity, it would nevertheless be desirable for the accounts of the charity for that year to be audited by such a person as is mentioned in that subsection,

the Commissioners may by order require the accounts of the charity for that year to be audited by such a person as is mentioned in that subsection.

5. If the Commissioners make an order under subsection 4 above with respect to a charity, then unless –

(a) the order is made by virtue of paragraph (b) of that subsection, and

(b) the charity trustees themselves appoint an auditor in accordance with the order, the auditor shall be a person appointed by the Commissioners.

6. The expenses of any audit carried out by an auditor appointed by the Commissioners under subsection 5 above, including the auditor's remuneration, shall be recoverable by the Commissioners –

(a) from the charity trustees of the charity concerned, who shall be personally liable, jointly and severally, for those expenses; or

(b) to the extent that it appears to the Commissioners not to be practical to seek recovery of those expenses in accordance with paragraph (a) above, from the funds of the charity.

7. The Commissioners may –

(a) give guidance to charity trustees in connection with the selection of a person for appointment as an independent examiner;

(b) give such directions as they think appropriate with respect to the carrying out of an examination in pursuance of subsection 3(a) above;

and any such guidance or directions may either be of general application or apply to a particular charity only.

8. The Secretary of State may by order amend subsection 1 or 3 above by substituting a different sum for the sum for the time being specified there.

9. Nothing in this section applies to a charity which is a company.

Section 44 (Supplementary provisions relating to audits, etc.) (see Rule 54(1))

1. The Secretary of State may by regulations make provision –

(a) specifying one or more bodies for the purposes of section 43(2)(b) above;

(b) with respect to the duties of an auditor carrying out an audit under section 43 above, including provision with respect to the making by him of a report on –

    (i) the statement of accounts prepared for the financial year in question under section 42(1) above, or

    (ii) the account and statement so prepared under section 42(3) above,

as the case may be;

(c) with respect to the making by an independent examiner of a report in respect of an examination carried out by him under section 43 above;

(d) conferring on such an auditor or on an independent examiner a right of access with respect to books, documents and other records (however kept) which relate to the charity concerned;

(e) entitling such an auditor or an independent examiner to require, in the case of a charity, information and explanations from past or present charity trustees or trustees for the charity, or from past or present officers or employees of the charity;

(f) enabling the Commissioners, in circumstances specified in the regulations, to dispense with the requirements of section 43(2) or (3) above in the case of a particular charity or in the case of any particular financial year of a charity.

2. If any person fails to afford an auditor or an independent examiner any facility to which he is entitled by virtue of subsection 1(d) or (e) above, the Commissioners may by order give –

(a) to that person, or

(b) to the charity trustees for the time being of the charity concerned, such directions as the Commissioners think appropriate for securing that the default is made good.

3. Section 727 of the Companies Act 1985 (power of court to grant relief in certain cases) shall have effect in relation to an auditor or independent examiner appointed by a charity in pursuance of section 43 above as it has effect in relation to a person employed as auditor by a company within the meaning of that Act.

NOTES

Part II Parochial Church Meetings and Councils

1 Under this section this report shall be delivered to the parochial church council at its meeting next before the annual parochial church meeting and, with such amendments as that council may make, to the ensuing annual parochial church meeting.

2 The Church Accounting Regulations 1997 to 2001, made by the General Synod, came into force in their amended form on 1 January 2002.

3 See Supplementary material (pp. 84–5) for the relevant text of this enactment.

Part IV Diocesan Synods

1 Under paragraph 4 of the Schedule to the Diocesan Boards of Education Measure 1991 the chairman of the Diocesan Board of Education is also an ex-officio member of the diocesan synod.

2 Under paragraph 4 of the Schedule to the Diocesan Boards of Education Measure 1991 the chairman of the Diocesan Board of Education is also an ex-officio member of the diocesan synod.

3 See Supplementary material (pp. 85–6) for the relevant text of this enactment.

4 See Supplementary material (pp. 85–6) for the relevant text of this enactment.

5 See Supplementary material (pp. 85–6) for the relevant text of this enactment.

6 See Supplementary material (p. 86) for the relevant text of this enactment.

Part V House of Laity of General Synod

1 See Supplementary material (p. 86) for the relevant text of this enactment.

2 See Supplementary material (p. 86) for the relevant text of this enactment.

Part VI Appeals and Disqualifications

1 See Supplementary material (pp. 82–4) for the relevant text of this enactment.

2 See Supplementary material (p. 82) for the relevant text of this enactment.

Part VII Supplementary and Interpretation

1 See Supplementary material (p. 87) for the relevant text of this enactment.

2 See Supplementary material (p. 87) for the relevant text of this enactment.

3 The Church Accounting Regulations 1997 to 2001, made by the General Synod, came into force in their amended form on 1 January 2002.

Appendix II General Provisions Relating to Parochial Church Councils

1 See Supplementary material (pp. 88–9) for the relevant text of this enactment.

Index

Note: the abbreviation PCC is used for Parochial Church Council.

adjournment
    of annual parochial meeting 11
    of meeting of parishioners 85
    of PCC meeting 80
age
    for election to deanery synod 11, 27
    for election to diocesan synod 34
    for election to General Synod 41, 42, 47
    for election to PCC 11
    for entry in electoral roll 1, 65, 67, 68, 70
agenda, PCC 78, 79
annual parochial church meeting
    see parochial church meeting
appeals
    costs 53
    election 13, 50–53, 59
    electoral roll 2, 49
Appointments Committee 52
archbishop 32, 62, 64, 86
Archbishops' Council 47
    employment by 56
archdeacon
    access to PCC minutes 80
    and diocesan synods 32
    and extraordinary parochial meeting 25
area synod 27, 38
    and election to General Synod 43
attendance, habitual 1–2, 7, 27, 30, 34, 43, 53–4, 66, 67
auditor 10, 63, 78, 80, 81, 86–9

benefice, held in plurality 8, 16, 20–22
    vacancy in 8, 77, 79
bishop
    access to PCC minutes 80
    and diocesan synod 32, 33, 35–6, 38–9, 62
    and pastoral breakdown in parish 82
    and special provisions 61
bishop's council
    and casual vacancies 58–9
    and deanery synods 28, 31, 33
    and diocesan synod 55, 58, 86
    and election appeals 52, 55
    and electoral roll decisions 1, 49–50
    functions 39
    matters referred from General Synod 86
    and payment of presiding officers 46
    and PCCs 19, 21, 23
bishop's licence 9, 26, 27, 63
boundaries, parochial 5
Business Committee of General Synod 42, 46, 64

canons, residentiary 30
Canterbury (province)
    and diocese in Europe 40, 62
    lay members of General Synod 41, 42
    Vicar-General 47, 51
Care of Churches and Ecclesiastical Jurisdiction Measure 1991 10
cathedral
    definition 64
    representation of clergy and laity 30, 42–3, 54
    see also community roll
Cathedrals Measure 1999 30
Central Board of Finance
    Chairman 47
    employment by 56

chairman
  of deanery synod 30, 45, 48, 50, 52
  of diocesan synod 38, 50, 52
  of extraordinary parochial meeting 25
  and General Synod House of Laity 50–52, 58
  of parochial church meeting 9, 10
  of PCC 6, 15, 18, 77–80
chancellor of diocese 32, 33
Channel Islands, General Synod members 41
Channel Islands (Representation) Measure 1931 41
chaplaincies, of diocese in Europe 41, 51, 55, 63
Charities Act 1960 82
Charities Act 1992 82, 84
Charities Act 1993 56, 63, 70, 74, 81, 82–4, 86–9
charity, ecclesiastical 55, 70, 74
Charity Commissioners 56, 70, 74, 81, 82–4, 87–9
Christ Church cathedral, Oxford 30, 34, 43
Church Accounting Regulations 90
Church Commissioners, employment by 56
Church of England
  churches in communion with 1, 63–4, 65–6, 67, 68
  relationship with other churches 86
Church of England Pensions Board 47
  employment by 56
Church Estates Commissioners 47
churchwarden
  casual vacancy 85
  deputy 19
  disqualification 55, 70, 82, 84
  elections 14, 50, 84
  and electoral roll 2
  and PCC membership 16
  as treasurer 77
Churchwardens Measure 2001 14, 84–5

City of London (Guild Churches) Acts 6
clergy
  in group ministry 8, 16
  in team ministry 7–8, 15, 16, 22
  see also clerk in Holy Orders; minister
Clerical Disabilities Act 1870 64
Clerical Disabilities Act 1870 (Amendment) Measure 1934 64
clerk of annual parochial meeting 11
Clerk to General Synod 46
clerk in Holy Orders
  and annual parochial meeting 7, 12
  and chairing of PCC meeting 79
  and deanery synod 26–7, 28
  and deed of relinquishment 64
  and diocesan synod 32–3, 34
  and membership of PCC 15
  and removal from electoral roll 3, 49
  and special parochial meeting 25
commissary 62
communicants
  and deanery synod membership 11, 27
  definition 63, 70
  and diocesan synod membership 33, 34
  and General Synod membership 40, 41, 42, 47
  and PCC membership 11, 15
communities, religious
  and diocesan synod 32, 33
  and General Synod 40, 41, 47
community roll 30, 34, 43, 53–4
Companies Act 1985 88
Company Directors Disqualification Act 1986 82
consent to serve 11, 36, 44, 58–9, 84
conventional district 63
Convocation of Canterbury 40
Convocations
  employment by 56
  Lower House 32
co-option
  to deanery synod 27–8, 29, 31, 34, 40
  to diocesan synod 33, 35

Index

to General Synod 33, 40, 47–8
to PCC 7, 15–16, 77
Corporation of the Church House 56
curates 22, 24, 63

deaconess
  and deanery synod 27, 28
  and group council 24
  and PCC membership 15
  and team council 22
Dean of the Arches and Auditor 47, 52
dean of cathedral 30, 32
deanery synod 26–31
  casual vacancies 57
  and cathedral clergy and laity 30, 42–3, 53
  co-opted members 27–8, 29, 31, 34, 40
  and diocesan synod 26, 27, 28–9, 30–31
  and disqualification 54
  and elections for diocesan synod 33, 34–7
  and elections for General Synod 40
  election to 2, 6, 10–11, 13–14, 28–9
  and General Synod members 26, 27
  membership 26–8
  number of meetings 30
  number of members 28–9
  officers *see* chairman; secretary
  and PCC membership 15, 17
  procedure 30–31
  qualifications of persons elected to 11–12
  reports to annual parochial meeting 10, 30, 69
  reports to PCC 30
  standing committee 30, 55
  term of office 28
  variation of membership 29
deed of relinquishment 64
definitions 63–4
deputy churchwarden 15, 18
deputy registrar, diocesan 34, 39

diocesan advisory committee 32, 33
diocesan board of finance 10, 32, 33, 53
Diocesan Boards of Education Measure 1991 90
diocesan electoral registration officer 13, 27, 28, 31, 36, 44, 49, 57
Diocesan record office 80
diocesan synod 32–9
  casual vacancies 34, 37, 54–5, 57, 59
  co-opted members 33, 35
  and deanery synod 26, 27, 28–9, 30–31
  and disqualification 74
  election appeals 50
  and elections to General Synod 40, 43, 58
  election to 2, 6, 33, 34–7, 72
  ex-officio members 32–3
  matters referred from General Synod 38, 86
  membership 32–4
  nomination form 73
  notice of election to 72
  number of meetings 38
  number of members 35
  and PCCs 15, 17
  procedure 38–9
  standing orders 38, 39, 86
  term of office 34
  variation of membership 37
  voting paper 75–6
diocese, as electoral area 43
diocese in Europe
  and archbishop of Canterbury 62
  and General Synod 41, 50, 51, 55
  matters referred from General Synod 86
  and province of Canterbury 40
Dioceses Measure 1978 27, 38
disqualification 16, 53–6, 70, 74, 82
district church councils 18–20, 56, 70

Ecclesiastical Fees Measure 1986 46
election addresses 36, 45

93

elections
  appeals 13, 50–56, 59
  of churchwardens 14, 50
  constraints 60
  to deanery synod 2, 6, 10–11, 13–14, 27, 28–9
  to diocesan synod 2, 6, 33, 34–7
  expenses 36, 44
  to General Synod 2, 6, 43–6
  to PCC 10, 13–14
  variation of method 13–14
electoral roll
  and access to PCC minutes 80
  addition of names 2, 5
  and annual parochial meeting 3–5, 7
  appeals 2, 49
  application form 1, 65–6
  certification of numbers 6
  community roll 30, 34, 43, 53–4
  and deanery synod membership 2, 6, 54
  and diocesan synod membership 2, 6, 34, 54
  display 3, 4, 5–6, 10, 67
  entry in more than one parish 1–2, 33, 47–48
  errors in 51
  failure to maintain 61–2
  formation 1–3
  and General Synod membership 2, 6, 42–3
  of guild church 6
  inspection 1, 67
  new 1, 4–5, 7, 9, 16, 66, 68
  and PCC membership 12, 15–16
  removal of names 2–3, 5, 49
  revision 1, 2, 3–4, 67
  and special parochial meetings 24
electoral roll officer 2, 6, 67, 68, 77–8
electors, names and addresses 36, 44–5
electronic mail 45, 78
employment, paid, and disqualification 54, 56
Episcopal Ministry Act of Synod 1993 33

examiner, independent 10, 63, 78, 80, 81, 86–9
ex-officio membership
  of diocesan synod 32–3
  and disqualification 56
  General Synod 33, 40, 47
  of PCC 15, 18
  of PCC standing committee 80
expenses
  of appeals 53
  of audit by Charity Commissioners 87–8
  of elections 36, 44
Extra-Parochial Ministry Measure 1967 26
extra-parochial place 1, 26

fabric, report on 10, 69
facsimile transmission of papers 36, 44, 45
financial statements (PCC) 10, 18, 69, 80, 81, 86–9
Forces Synodical Council 40
form, valid 61

General Synod
  Business Committee 42, 46, 64
  casual vacancies 41, 42, 57–8
  conduct of elections 43–6
  Constitution 34, 47, 48
  co-opted members 33, 40, 47–8
  and disqualifications 54–6
  election appeals 50–52
  and elections to diocesan synods 37
  and elections to PCCs 13
  electoral areas 42
  employment by 56
  ex-officio members 33, 40, 47
  House of Laity 2, 6, 40–48, 50–52, 54–5, 57
  matters referred to diocesan synods 38, 86
  members on deanery synods 26, 27
  members on diocesan synods 34

number of elected members 41–2
and PCC membership 15
presiding officers 46–7
qualifications of elected members 42–3
and relationship with other churches 86
Standing Orders 43, 45, 64
term of office 47
and variation in deanery synod membership 29
group council 24
group ministry
and annual parochial meeting 8
and PCCs 16
guild church, electoral roll 6

house of bishops, of diocesan synod 29, 32, 38
house of clergy
of deanery synod 26–7, 29, 31, 33, 34–6, 54
of diocesan synod 29, 32–3, 38, 49, 50, 52, 62, 72, 73, 75–6
house of laity
of deanery synod 26, 27, 29, 30, 31, 33, 34–6, 40, 54
of diocesan synod 29, 32, 33, 38, 49, 50, 55, 72, 73, 75–6
of General Synod 33, 40–48, 50–52, 54–6, 57

incumbents 63
and breakdown of pastoral relationship 82
and PCC membership 16
see also clergy; minister
Incumbents (Vacation of Benefices) Measure 1977 56, 70, 82
independent examiner 10, 63, 78, 80, 81, 86–9
Insolvency Act 1986 82

joint PCCs 20–22

laity, definition 63
Law Reform (Miscellaneous Provisions) (Scotland) Act 1990 83
lay worker
and deanery synod 27, 28
and group council 24
and PCC membership 15
and team council 22
licence, bishop's 9, 26, 27, 63
Local Government Act 1894 56, 70, 74
lot, selection by 13, 17, 37

mail, electronic 45, 78
minister
and annual parochial meeting 8, 9
as chairman of PCC 15, 77, 81
definition 63
and election of churchwardens 84–5
and electoral roll 2, 3–4
and joint council 20

nominations 12, 36, 44, 84
form 36, 73
notice
of annual parochial meeting 8, 69–70
of diocesan synod election 72
of PCC meeting 78–9
of resignation 60

parish
alteration of boundaries 5
definition 64, 66
with more than one place of worship 2–3, 18–20
new 2, 8–9
parishioners, meeting to elect a churchwarden 85
Parochial Church Council *see* PCC
parochial church meeting
annual 7–14
business 9–11
casting votes 9
chairman 9, 10
clerk 11

conduct of elections 12–13
convening 8–9
date 7, 8
election of churchwardens 14
elections to deanery synod 6, 10–11, 13, 27, 28
elections to PCC 10
and electoral roll 3–5, 7, 9, 69–70
failure to hold 61–2
and joint PCCs 20–22
notice of 8, 69–70
parishes with more than one place of worship 18–20
qualifications of person chosen or elected by 11–12
and team councils 22–3
and team ministry 7–8
extraordinary 25
special 9, 11, 19, 21, 23, 25
Parochial Registers and Records Measure 1978 80
Pastoral Measure 1983 19, 21, 22, 24, 78
pastoral schemes
and annual parochial meeting 8–9
and electoral roll 2
and group council 24
and joint PCCs 20–22
and PCC membership 16, 19
and team clergy 63
and team council 23
Patronage (Benefices) Measure 1986 19, 20, 23, 24
payment
of independent examiner or auditor 78
of presiding officer 46
of secretary of PCC 77
of treasurer of PCC 78
PCC 15–24
adjournment of meetings 80
agendas 78, 79
annual reports 9–10, 69
casual vacancies 17, 57
committees 81

co-opted members 7, 15–16, 77
deanery synod members 15, 17
and deanery synod reports 30, 69
and disqualifications 16, 55, 70, 82
and district church council 18–20, 55, 70
elections to 10, 14
and electoral roll 4
emergency meeting 79
ex-officio members 15, 18
failure to maintain 61–2
financial statements 10, 18, 69, 80, 81, 86–9
general provisions 17, 77–81
and group councils 24
joint 20–21
limitation on years of service 18
membership 2, 11, 15–16
minutes 77, 80
notice of meeting 78–9
number of meetings 78
officers *see* chairman; electoral roll officer; secretary; treasurer; vice-chairman
place of meeting 80
qualifications of persons elected to 11–12
and quorum for meeting 79
standing committee 80–81
and team councils 22–3
term of office 15, 17
validity of proceedings 81
Pensions Board 47
employment by 56
plurality of benefices 8, 16, 20–22
postal votes 14, 70, 71
presiding officer
and constraints in elections 60
for deanery synod elections 31
for diocesan synod elections 36, 37, 75–6
and fresh elections 59
for General Synod elections 44–7, 51, 58–9

for parochial church meeting 14
  payment 46
priest-in-charge 63
Priests (Ordination of Women) Measure 1993 19, 21, 23, 24
proceedings, validity 61, 81
proctors 32, 86
provincial episcopal visitor 33–4
provost of cathedral 30, 32

quorum, for PCC meeting 79

readers, and PCC membership 15
rector, in team ministry 9, 22, 24, 78
register
  of clerical electors 31, 34–5, 49, 51
  of lay electors 31, 34–5, 41, 44, 51
registrar, diocesan 34, 39, 44
registrar, provincial 44, 46
Rehabilitation of Offenders Act 1974 82
relinquishment, deed of 64
residence 64
  and entry in electoral roll 1
resignation 59–60
revocation of rules 60–61
rules
  revocation and variation 60–61
  and special provisions 61–2
rural dean 27, 30, 45, 61–2

St George's Chapel, Windsor 30, 32, 34, 43, 64
scrutineer, for General Synod elections 46
seconding of nominations 12, 36, 44, 84
secretary
  of deanery synod 13, 27, 28, 30, 31, 35, 44, 57, 77
  of diocesan synod 6, 28, 35, 37, 38, 41, 77
  of PCC 6, 8, 11, 13, 28, 57, 77–9
sidesmen, appointment 10, 11, 70
Sodor and Man, Diocese 41
standing committee
  of deanery synod 30, 55

  of diocesan synod *see* bishop's council
  of General Synod House of Laity 47
  of PCC 80–81
standing orders
  of diocesan synod 38, 39, 86
  of General Synod 43, 45, 48, 64
suffragan bishop 32, 33–4
Synodical Government Measure 1969 38–9, 63, 85–6

team ministry
  and annual parochial meeting 7–8, 9
  and district church councils 19–20
  and PCC membership 15, 16, 20
  and team councils 22–3
  and vicars 7–8, 9, 16, 24, 63, 78
treasurer, of PCC 77–8, 81
trustee, charity 87–9
  disqualification 55, 70, 74, 82–4

universities, and diocesan synod membership 32

vacancy
  in archbishopric 62
  in benefice 8, 77, 79
  in bishopric 62
vacancy, casual 57–9, 61
  for churchwarden 85
  for deanery synod 57
  for diocesan synod 34, 37, 54–5, 57, 59
  for General Synod 41, 42, 57–8
  for PCC 17, 57
  through disqualification 54–5
variation of rules 60–61
vicar, in team ministry 7–8, 9, 16, 24, 63, 78
Vicars-General of Provinces 47, 52
vice-chairman
  and General Synod House of Laity 50–52
  of PCC 6, 8, 9, 70, 77, 79

voting
  casting vote 9, 38, 80
  counting of votes 45–6
  equal division of 9, 13, 37, 38, 80, 85
  by houses 30, 38, 86
  by majority 80, 86
  postal 14, 70, 71
  recounts 13, 46
  by show of hands 12
  by single transferable vote 13, 45, 76

voting papers 12, 13, 14, 36–7, 45, 58, 75–6

Westminster Abbey 30, 32, 34, 43, 65
worshipper, habitual 1–2, 7, 27, 30, 34, 43, 53–4, 66, 67
worship, public 63

York (province)
  lay members of General Synod 41, 42
  Vicar-General 47, 51